Step Out on Nothing

How Faith and Family Helped Me Conquer Life's Challenges

BYRON PITTS

ST. MARTIN'S GRIFFIN NEW YORK

This is a true story, though a few names
and details have been changed.

www.stmartins.com

Book design by Phil Mazzone

The Library of Congress has cataloged the
hardcover edition as follows:

Pitts, Byron.
    Step out on nothing : how family and faith helped me conquer life's
challenges / Byron Pitts.—1st ed.
        p. cm.
    ISBN 978-0-312-57766-7
    1. Pitts, Byron.   2. Baptists—United States—Biography.   3. Television
journalists—United States—Biography.   I. Title.
    BX6455.P38A3 2009
    277.3'082092—dc22
    [B]
                                                            2009019891

ISBN 978-0-312-57999-9 (trade paperback)

10   9   8   7   6   5   4   3

To my mother, Clarice Pitts;
my sister, Saundra Judd;
and my brother, William M. Pitts.
God's brought us a mighty long way.

Contents

CONTENTS

Introduction

New York City

In five, four, three, two . . ." This wasn't the first time a floor director had ever counted me down, but it was the first time I ever choked back tears. It was August 25, 2006, my first on-camera studio open for the CBS News broadcast *60 Minutes*. Moments earlier I'd been in makeup with famed artist Riccie Johnson. She'd done up the likes of Mike Wallace, Harry Reasoner, Morley Safer, Dan Rather, Ed Bradley, Lesley Stahl, Steve Kroft, and every other big-name correspondent who ever worked for *60 Minutes*. And the Beatles. And now she was putting powder on *me*.

Executive Producer Jeff Fager poked his head in the dressing room, "Good luck, Brotha! You've come a long way to get here. You've earned it." I think Jeff was talking about my ten years of covering hurricanes, tornadoes, politics, the September 11 disaster, wars in Afghanistan and Iraq, and every other sort of story for *CBS News* during those years.

If he only knew. My mind flashed back to elementary school, when a therapist had informed my mother, "I'm sorry, Mrs. Pitts, your son is functionally illiterate. He cannot read."

Months earlier, another so-called expert had suggested I was mentally retarded. Perhaps there was a "special needs" program right for me. Here I was some three decades later sitting in the "special" chair of the most revered show in the history of broadcast news. Musicians dream of playing Carnegie Hall, astronauts work a lifetime to take their first mission in space, and every broadcast journalist worth his or her salt dreams of *60 Minutes*.

Engineers generally keep television studios icy cold to prevent the equipment from overheating. The *60 Minutes* studio is no different. But in this age of high-tech sets with massive video walls and graphic trickery, Studio 33, where *60 Minutes* is taped, looks more like a throwback. You can almost smell the cigar smoke from decades past. Black-covered walls. Bright lights hanging from the ceiling. There's one camera and one chair. As a correspondent, you sit in the chair, cross your legs, look into the camera, and tell a story.

"Take two. In three, two, one!"

Seven takes later I finally recorded one that everybody liked. It took a while—not so much to settle my nerves as to get everyone settled in that one chair. Sitting with me were my mother, Clarice Pitts; my grandmother, Roberta Mae Walden; my sister, Saundra; and my brother, Mac. We had made the journey as a family, with the help of a few friends and even a few strangers.

What an overwhelming feeling it was and the symbolism was not lost on me.

That afternoon, to all who could see, I was seated alone. But I knew better. Some thirty-seven years before I would ever hear the phrase "Step Out on Nothing," God was writing those words to cover my life. How many times has each of us been in a difficult place and thought we were alone? Standing on nothing. Perhaps it is only in the empty space of those moments we can truly feel God's breath at our necks. His hands beneath our feet. Step out on nothing? Yes. Step out on faith.

So where did I get the title for this book? *Step Out on Nothing*. What does it mean and how does it fit into my life? Most important, how do you find the courage to try it?

I first heard those fateful words on a Sunday in March of 2007, Women's Day at St. Paul Baptist Church in Montclair, New Jersey. My wife was excited. She'd helped with the weekend program. Me, not so much. As usual I was running late for service and she was getting annoyed. We arrived at church in time. The place was packed. Women all dressed in white and black. The guest preacher that morning was Reverend Benita Lewis. She began her sermon by talking about the pain women will endure to be beautiful. She talked about pedicures, high-heeled shoes, and women's sore feet. I thought to myself, *This is going to be a long service*. Nothing here for me. And it got worse. She moved from pedicures to massages and spa treatments. Body wraps to skin treatments. At that point I was drifting away. It felt as if we'd been in church for hours. But Reverend Lewis was just warming up, and I soon discovered that she wasn't speaking only to the women in the congregation. She was telling all of us about overcoming pain and obstacles in our paths. She was talking about a belief in God, a faith so strong that anything is possible. Then Reverend Lewis uttered four words that took my breath away. "Step out on nothing." She encouraged the congregation to "step out on faith" in this journey we call life. To put your life and its challenges in God's hands. To believe in a power greater than yourself.

Step out . . . on nothing . . .

In the time it takes to say those four words, a lifetime flashed before me. She was speaking about my life. How had I overcome my childhood inability to read when I was nearly a teenager? It was my mother stepping out on nothing, despite the doubts she must have had during the nights around the kitchen table when I "just wasn't getting it."

And how do you explain an inner-city kid who stuttered until he was twenty years old becoming a network television news correspondent? Let's start with a college professor who didn't even know my name. She stepped out on nothing and believed in a young man who didn't believe in himself.

Then there's Peter Holthe: a stranger. A college classmate from Minnetonka, Minnesota. "Why's your vocabulary so limited?" he asked. He stayed around to find out why and helped expand it.

Those Franciscan Friars at Archbishop Curley High School in Baltimore, Maryland, who heard I was in a gospel choir at a church across town. These were white men who'd never ventured into a black neighborhood or set foot in a Baptist church. They too stepped out on nothing, figuring that being supportive of one of their students after hours might actually make a difference in his life.

We all have those defining moments in our lives. Moments of great joy. Moments of unspeakable sadness and fear. We usually think we're alone. But if we look into the corners of our memories, we'll find them—those people who had faith in us. Those times when a grace beyond earthly understanding touches us.

This is a story of those times. Those people. And the lessons they taught me. We've all had such people in our lives. If not, it's time to find them.

And for me, this story is my "step out on nothing," revealing a childhood shame that I've hidden from all but those who are closest to me, in hopes that my leap of faith will inspire some young child, or even an adult, who is living with a secret. It took me years to discover my shame was actually a source of strength.

ONE

Mustard Seed Faith—With It You Can Move Mountains

Because you have so little faith, I tell you the truth, if you have faith as small as a mustard seed, you can say to this mountain, "Move from here to there," and it will move. Nothing will be impossible for you.

—Matthew 17:20

1969 Baltimore

At age nine I was a fourth-grader in a Catholic school, and the only whore I had ever heard of was the lady in the Bible. That was until one day when, dressed in my school uniform of blue pants, white shirt, and gray and blue striped tie, my mom picked me up and we set out on one of the defining adventures of my young life.

"Get in the car! We're going to that whore's house!"

It couldn't have been more than a ten-minute ride. My mother, who loves to talk, never said a word. We drove up on a busy street lined with row houses, each tipped with Baltimore's famed three-marble steps. I've never considered my mom an athlete, but that day she pushed at the driver's side door like a sprinter leaping off the starting block and quickly made her way to a house with a narrow door and a small diamond-shaped window. She rang the doorbell several times. A pretty woman with long curly brown hair finally answered the door. I was struck by how much she resembled my mother.

"Tell my husband to come out here," my mother yelled.

The woman answered, "I don't know what you're talking about" and slammed the door.

I could see the rage building in my mother's fists and across her face. She backed off the steps and screamed toward a window on the second floor,

"William Pitts! You son of a bitch! Bring your ass outside right now!"

There was dead silence. So she said it again. Louder. If no one inside that house could hear her, the neighbors did. People on the street stopped moving; others started coming out of their homes. My mom had an audience. I stood near the car, paralyzed by shame. Figuring it was her message and not her volume, my mother came up with a new line.

"William Pitts! You son of a bitch! You come outside right now or I will set your car on fire!"

He apparently heard her that time. Much to my surprise, my father, dressed only in his pants and undershirt, dashed out of that house as my mother made her way to his car. She ordered me to move away from her car and get into my father's car. I did. My father was barefoot, and he slipped as he approached my mother. She picked up a brick and took dead aim at my father's head. She missed. He ran to the other side of his car. She retrieved the brick and tried again. She missed. He ran. My parents repeated their version of domestic dodge ball at least a half dozen times. It must have seemed like a game to the gallery of people who watched and laughed. I never said a word. In the front passenger seat of my father's car, I kept my eyes straight ahead. I didn't want to watch, though I couldn't help but hear. My parents were fighting again, and this time in public.

Eventually, my father saw an opening and jumped into the driver's seat of his car. Fumbling for his keys, he failed to close the door. My mother jumped on top of him. Cursing and scratching at his eyes and face, she seemed determined to kill him. I could see her fingers inside his mouth. Somehow my father's head ended up in my lap. The scratches on his face began to bleed onto my white shirt. For the first time since my mother picked me up from school, I spoke. Terrified, I actually screamed.

"Why! What did I do? Wha-wa-wa-wa-wut!"

I'm sure I had more to say, but I got stuck on the word *what*. Almost from the time I could speak, I stuttered. It seemed to get worse when I was frightened or nervous. Sitting in my dad's car with my parents' weight and their problems pressed against me, I stuttered and cried. It seemed odd to me at that moment, but as quickly and violently as my parents began fighting, they stopped. I guess it was my mother who first noticed the blood splattered across my face and soaked through my shirt. She thought I was bleeding. In that instant, the temperature cooled in the car. It had been so hot. My parents' body heat had caused the three of us to sweat. Fearing they had injured me, my parents tried to console me. But once they stopped fighting, I did what I always seemed to do. I put on my mask. I closed my mouth and pretended everything was all right.

I was used to this—there had been a lot of secrets in our house. My father had been hiding his infidelity. Both parents were putting a good face on marital strife for their family and friends. You see, almost from the time Clarice and William Pitts met, he was unfaithful. Women on our street, in church, those he'd meet driving a cab, and the woman who would eventually bear him a child out of wedlock. I have only known her as Miss Donna. Clarice may have despised the woman, but if ever her name came up in front of the children, she was Miss Donna. The car ride was a tortured awakening for me, but it was just the beginning. The picture our family showed the outside world was beginning to unravel, and when all our secrets began to spill into the open, on the street, in the classroom, and in our church, none of our lives would ever be the same.

My mother was accustomed to hard times. Clarice Pitts was a handsome woman, with thick strong hands, a square jaw, cold gray eyes, and a love for her children bordering on obsession. Her philosophy was always: "If you work hard and pray hard and treat people right, good things will happen." That was her philosophy. Unfortunately, that was not her life.

Clarice was the second of seven children born in a shotgun house in the segregated South of Apex, North Carolina, on January 1, 1934. By mistake, the doctor wrote Clarence Walden on her birth certificate, and until the age of twelve, when she went for her Social Security card, the world thought my mother was a man. Truth be told, for three-quarters of a century, she's been tougher than most men you'd meet. Her father, Luther Walden, was by all accounts a good provider and a bad drinker. He'd work the farm weekdays, work the bottle weekends. Her mother, Roberta Mae, was both sweet and strong. Friends nicknamed her Señorita because she was always the life of the party, even after back-breaking work. All the kids adored their mother and feared their father. On more than a few occasions, after he'd been drinking all day, her father would beat his wife and chase the children into the woods.

At sixteen, Clarice thought marriage would be better than living at home, where she was afraid to go to sleep at night when her father had been drinking. So she married a man nearly twice her age (he was twenty-nine), and they had one child, my sister, Saundra Jeannette Austin. People thought that since Clarice married a man so much older she would have a ton of babies. But she was never one to conform to others' expectations. She promised herself never to have more children than she could care for, or a husband that she couldn't tolerate. He never raised his hand to her. He did, however, have a habit of raising a liquor bottle to his mouth. She divorced him three years later, and by the mid-1950s she and my sister had started a new life in Baltimore, Maryland, which held the promise of a better education and a better job than was available to her in the South.

She finally thought life had given her a break when she met William Archie Pitts. They met in night school. "He was a real flirt, but smart," she said. In 1958 William A. Pitts could have been Nat King Cole's taller younger brother. He was jet black with broad shoulders; his uniform of choice a dark suit, dark tie, crisp white shirt, a white cotton pocket-square, and polished shoes. He dressed like a preacher, spoke like a hustler, and worked as a butcher. Clarice looked good on his arm and liked being there even more. He was ebony. She was ivory, or as Southerners said back then, she was "high yellow." My father had been married once before as well. His first wife died in childbirth, and he was raising their son on his own.

After a whirlwind romance of steamed crabs on paper tablecloths and dances at the local Mason lodge, the two married. A short time later, I was born on October 21, 1960. There was no great family heritage or biblical attachment associated with my name. They chose my name out of a baby book. My mother simply liked the sound of it. One of the few indulgences of her life in the early 1960s was dressing her baby boy like John F. Kennedy Jr. She kept me in short pants as long as she could. She finally relented when I started high school. Just kidding. But to me it certainly felt as if she held on until the last possible moment.

Life held great promise for William and Clarice Pitts in the 1960s. The year after I was born, Clarice finished high school and later graduated college the year before my sister earned her first of several degrees. She worked in a few different sewing factories in Baltimore. She took on side jobs making hats for women at church and around the city. Both of my parents believed God had given them a second chance. Almost instantly William and Clarice Pitts had a family: two boys and a daughter. My parents bought their first and only home together at 2702 East Federal Street.

Outsiders knew my hometown as just Baltimore, but if you grew up there, there were actually two Baltimores; East Baltimore and West Baltimore. And the side of the city you lived on said as much about you as your last name or your parents' income. East Baltimore was predominantly blue collar, made up mostly of cement, ethnic neighborhoods, and tough-minded people. Most people I knew worked with their hands and worked hard for their money. You loved family, your faith, the Colts, and the Orioles. In 1969 my world centered on the 2700 block of East Federal Street. Ten blocks of red brick row houses, trimmed with aluminum siding. Decent people kept their furniture covered in plastic. Each house had a patch of grass out front. To call it a lawn would be too generous. The yards on East Federal were narrow and long, like the hood of the Buick Electric 225 my father drove. Those in the know called that model car a Deuce and a Quarter. Ours was a neighborhood on the shy side of working class. Like I said, my father was a meat cutter at the local meat plant. My mother was a seamstress at the London Fog coat factory. My sister was about to graduate from high school. Big hair. Bigger personality. I idolized her. My brother was sixteen. We had the typical big brother–little brother relationship: we hated each other. Born William MacLauren, we've always called him Mac as in MacLauren, but it could have stood for Mack truck. Not surprisingly, he grew up and became a truck driver. Even as a boy, he was built like a man, stronger than most, with a quiet demeanor that shouted "Fool with me at your own risk." He and Clarice Pitts were not blood relatives; however, they'd always shared a fighter's heart and a silent understanding that the world had somehow abandoned them. They would always have each other.

My nickname in the neighborhood was Pickle. I despised that name, but it seemed to fit. You know the big kid in the neighborhood? That wasn't me. I was thin as a coatrack, my head shaped like a rump roast covered in freckles. We were a Pepsi family, but my glasses resembled Coke bottles. I was shy out of necessity. But whatever my life lacked in 1969, football filled the void. I loved Johnny Unitas, John Mackey, and the Baltimore Colts. I never actually went to a game. I guess we couldn't afford it. But no kid in the stands ever adored that team more than I did.

On Federal Street, the Pitts kids had a reputation: God-fearing, hard-working, and polite. Next to perhaps breathing, few things have meant more to my mother than good manners. She'd often remark, when I was very young, and with great conviction and innocence, "If you never learn to read and write, you *will* be polite and work hard." Most days, that was enough. Back in North Carolina, the only reading materials around my grandmother's home were the Bible and *Ebony* magazine. My parents did one better with the Bible, *Ebony*, and *Jet*. My father read the newspaper. My mother had her schoolbooks, but reading and pleasure rarely shared the same space in our house. Neither one of my parents ever read to me, as best I can recall. We had a roof over our heads, food on the table, and church every Sunday. When my mother compared our lives to her childhood—in which she and some of her siblings actually slept in the woods on more than a few nights, terrified that their father would come home in a drunken rage and beat them—she felt that her children had it good.

Around the house, my mother was the enforcer, dishing out the discipline in our family. My father was the fun-loving life of the party and primary breadwinner. As long as I can remember, relatives from across the country (mostly the South) would call our home, seeking my mother's counsel. When there was trouble, people called Clarice. My dad loved cooking, telling stories, and occasionally, if encouraged, he would sing songs. The same relatives who often called my mom for advice would flock to our house annually to enjoy those times when my dad would cook their favorite foods, retell their favorite stories, and pour their favorite drinks. At some point in the evening, my mother would end up in my dad's lap, and neighbors could hear the laughter from our home pouring out onto the sidewalk. Those were the good days.

For better or worse, there was structure or, at the very least, a routine in the first years of my life. My mother made my brother and me get haircuts every Saturday. We enjoyed one style: The number one. The skinny. And my mother's favorite, "Cut it close." Food was part of the ritual too. We'd have pot roast for Sunday dinner. Leftovers on Monday, fried chicken on Tuesday, pork chops Wednesday, liver on Thursday (I hated liver, so I got salisbury steak), fish sticks on Friday, and "Go for yourself" on Saturday. But mealtime was often the flashpoint for the anger and bitterness that began to consume my parents' marriage. Their fight scene on the street was a rarity, but Fight Night at the Dinner Table, as the kids called it, was a regular feature. Meals always started with a prayer, "Heavenly Father, thank you for the food we're about to receive . . . ," and often ended early.

The fight usually started with very little warning, either my mother's sudden silence or my father's sarcasm. One night we were having fried pork chops (so it had to have been a

Wednesday). Pork chops were my favorite, with mashed potatoes and cabbage on the side, and blue Kool-Aid (that's grape to the uninitiated). The sounds of silverware against plates and light conversation filled the air. Then came the look. We all caught it at different times. My mother was staring a hole through my father's head. It sounded like she dropped her fork from the ceiling, but it actually fell no more than three inches from her hand to her plate. My dad gave his usual response soaked in innocence: "What?"

He didn't realize my mother had been listening on the phone in our kitchen when he had called Miss Donna from an upstairs phone to see how their son, Myron, was doing. Yes, I said their *son*. I think my mother was actually willing to forgive his child by another woman several years after my birth. But his name being so close to mine (Byron/Myron) was what seemed to break her heart and sometimes her spirit. At this point during dinner, however, she wasn't just broken— she was angry. First went her plate. Aimed at his head. And then her coffee cup. Then my plate. Followed rapid-fire by Mac's and Saundra's dinner plates.

"Calm down, Momma!" Saundra, the ring announcer, screamed.

Mac, always the referee, stood up to make sure no one went for a knife or scissors. Me? I just sat there. You ever notice at a prizefight, the people with the best seats don't move a lot? They're spellbound by the action in the ring. That was me at the kitchen table: left side, center seat between my parents, my brother and sister on the other side. That night my mother was determined, if not accurate. Four feet away, four tries, but my mother never hit my father once. Granted he was bobbing and weaving the whole time, like Cassius Clay dodging a Sonny Liston jab. As my father dodged plates and coffee cups, he would call my mother Sweetie. Her name of choice for him was Son of a Bitch. Except for a few potatoes in his hair, he got away without a scratch. The plates and the wallpaper didn't fare as well. With coffee-stained walls and cabinets full of chipped plates and broken utensils, I presumed every family had some variation on the same theme. And as quickly as it started, the fight was over. My father backpedaled to another room. My mother retreated to the comfort of her sewing machine. I cleared the table. My sister washed dishes. My brother dried them. We finished our homework. I was in bed by 8:30 P.M.

For all their bickering, Clarice and William Pitts always worked hard. They always believed in the power of prayer, the goodness of God's grace, and the importance of faith. That partially explains why my mother stayed married as long as she did. For as long as I can remember, she's worn a tiny mustard seed encased in a small plastic ball on a chain around her neck. The story of the mustard seed in the Bible has always given her great comfort.

Matthew 17:20: "Because you have so little faith, I tell you the truth, if you have faith as small as a mustard seed, you can say to this mountain, 'Move from here to there,' and it will move. Nothing will be impossible for you."

It's a belief that anything's possible if one's willing to work hard enough, if one's faith runs deep enough. I think she still believed in her marriage long after it was over. Her first answer to every difficult situation was always the same: "Did you pray yet?" In the midst of any crisis, whether at the beginning, the middle, or the end, my mother always turned to prayer. That night—after my parents fought on the street and my father bled inside his car on my lap, outside his girlfriend's house, where strangers looked on and laughed, in a neighborhood I'd never seen before but have never forgotten—my mother drove me home and we prayed.

We never said a word in the car on the way home. My mother had climbed off my father, held my hand, and scooted me into her car first. We went home in silence. I ate dinner in those same bloody clothes. I washed my hands but not my face. No one seemed to notice. The tension that evening had exhausted everyone. We all headed for bed early.

"Go take off those clothes and leave them outside your door," my mother told me. "Call me when you've got your pajamas on."

I did. I could hear her walking up the stairs. Slow and deliberate, as if she was carrying a heavy load. Earlier, back in my father's car, when I glanced into my mother's gray eyes, they were narrow and mean. Now at home, in my room, her eyes were soft around the edges and sad. My mother was not the crying type. She wasn't crying then. But she was sad. I could see it in the slump of her shoulders. It was written across her face.

"You okay?" she asked me. Her tone now was 180 degrees lighter than a few hours ago, when she had picked me up from school.

"What happened between me and your father had nothing to do with you," she said. "I wish we could wash away memories as easily as we can wash clothes," she added. Then she took my hands, closed her eyes, and touched her head to mine and started to pray. It's the way I've prayed ever since.

"Dear wise and almighty God, we come to you as humbly as we know how, just to say thank you, Lord. Thank you for blessings seen and unseen. Thank you, Lord, for our family, our friends, and even our enemies. Thank you, Lord, for the bad days, for they help us to better appreciate the good ones. Please, Lord, mend us where we are broken. Make us strong where we are weak. Give us, Lord, the faith to believe our tomorrow will be brighter than our yesterday. Hold us, Lord. Keep us in the palms of Your hands. Give us faith to keep holding on. These and all other blessings we ask in Jesus' name. Amen."

I opened my eyes to her familiar smile. We're not a teeth-smiling family—more grinners. But her grin promised better days were ahead. She hugged me. Tucked me in. Said good night. I remember expecting an apology before she left the room. After the day I'd had? Please! But *sorry* is not a word my mother used very often. The suggestion was, *sorry* indicated regret. With faith, why have regrets? Everything happens for a reason, for the good. Perhaps understanding would come by and by. As I listened to my mother's footsteps beyond my door, I suddenly felt a peace. The clanking of our old electric fan in the window even had a pleasant melody to it. On the surface, not a damn thing good had happened to me that day. But at that moment, after my mother's prayers, all I could think about was rejoicing in the notion that I was now on the other side of a difficult moment.

TWO

Keep Your Head Up

No good *thing* will be withheld from them that walk up-rightly.

—Psalm 84:11

Keep your head up no matter what. I heard that line so often as a child that I still hear it in my sleep. I've repeated it to colleagues, new acquaintances, even strangers. It was one of my mother's favorite expressions. It was a saying to motivate if needed and redirect if necessary. Keep your head up was never meant as a statement of false pride or arrogance. It was always one of Clarice's go-to phrases in difficult moments, meant to reverse whatever circumstance was pulling us down.

But honestly it was hard for me to keep my head up with so much weighing me down. While I was loved and spoiled, like the youngest child in many families, all that attention could not smooth over the deep flaws that I was hiding. Only my closest relatives, a few friends, and a teacher or two even knew I stuttered. But the big secret: *I couldn't read.* That was top secret. I was a phony, faking it, mouthing words in books that I did not really understand. Hiding my secret from my teachers and my parents. One of my favorite songs of the late 1960s was "Secret Agent Man." That was me carrying what seemed to me one of the great secrets in the world. I could not read, yet no one seemed to notice. It was a distressful combination for a boy who had big dreams. Illiterate *and* barely able to speak. I could read my name and a few simple words that I saw every day. It wasn't much, but for the time being it was enough. I was also unfailingly polite. In public school simply being polite all but guaranteed at least a passing grade in most classes. I was quiet and a good athlete. (I was never first pick as a class project partner, but if it was stick ball, football, or tag, Byron Pitts was a first-round draft pick.) All reasons enough for most teachers to leave me alone and for my peers to give me space. Most of my classes at Fort Worthington Elementary School, known simply as P.S. 85, were overcrowded. It's the same school my brother attended, and so in part I lived off his reputation. My brother was quiet, hard-working, and an average student. My mother was an active participant in parent activities. I was in a sense a legacy student, surviving at P.S. 85 on the family name. It was assumed I was learning, just as Mac had. For a quiet child falling further and further behind, it was a good place to not get noticed.

But I was performing well below average. In first and second grades, there was not a single A or B on my report card. My highest marks were always in behavior. My mother finally decided that the public school system was getting too big and impersonal for me. Because the discipline and attention offered in a parochial school was much more appealing to her, in September of 1968, for the third grade, she moved me to a Catholic school called St. Katharine's.

It didn't matter where I went, school was work, difficult work. And so, walking into St. Katharine's every morning felt like a job I wasn't good at and didn't enjoy. The school was a nondescript three-story cement building surrounded by a cast-iron fence on what appeared to be more like an alley than a street. There were row houses on three sides of the St. Katharine's Church building, which was later converted into a Baptist church, as the neighborhood continued to change. Most of the teachers were nuns. They treated me well. The strict discipline only seemed like an extension of Clarice's rules. It was actually comforting being in a school where nearly everyone was afraid of breaking the rules. There were never any more than twelve to fifteen kids in a class. Hardwood floors were polished to such a high sheen that you could see a reflection. The place had a clean, antiseptic smell. Giant windows were perfect for daydreaming about matters other than school. The boys wore uniform shirts, pants, and ties. The girls wore blue, gray, and white checked dresses. There was great emphasis on prayer and discipline. Reading, writing, and arithmetic seemed like second-tier priorities. Most of my classmates came from working-class homes, and many were raised by single parents. Despite our age, most of us seemed well aware that someone was sacrificing to send us to Catholic school. As usual, I became one of the less visible boys in class.

My third-grade teacher was Sister Clarice. I admit, I had a crush on her. She was the prettiest nun in our school. But that was just about the highlight of my school experience. In this new environment, being polite was no longer enough to get by. I could not read and understand sentences. Even simple ones. And the more difficult the work, the less I tried, the more easily I was distracted. We were required to read aloud at least once a week, and it was torture. Between the stammering and stuttering and mispronounced words, I was hard-pressed to do anything but hang my head in shame.

The only relief I had was that I was bright enough to memorize just about anything read to me. At night during homework time I would torture my family into helping me. A few tears every now and then would seal it. Since my sister was soon to be away at college, these after-dinner study sessions usually fell to my brother. Though our family lived in a three-bedroom home with a living room, dining room, kitchen, and almost-finished basement, we spent most of our time in the kitchen. That's where homework was done. (Perhaps that is why, to this day, I do my best thinking near food.) And it was one of the early front lines in my secret battle to hide my reading problems.

The two of us at the dinner table built for six. We'd sit across from each other. Table covered with our books, two glasses of milk, buttered toast or peanut butter sandwiches. Why buttered toast as an after-dinner homework snack? I have no clue, but it was what it was.

"Mac, help me please. Pretty please," I'd beg.

I was never sure if it was because my brother loved me so much, hated my whining more, or simply feared my mother's reaction if he didn't help, but whatever his motivation he'd suffer patiently.

"Okay! I'll read it to you one more time. Pay attention," he said, frustration wrinkling his forehead. Our study sessions could go on for three hours. Arithmetic, reading, spelling, history—it didn't matter the subject. Before the night was over, my brother would end up finishing my assignment and I'd have sections memorized for class.

In school the next day, when it came time to read aloud, I would have my section memorized. Sister Clarice took great pride in student involvement.

"Today we'll read chapter three."

Hands would shoot up. The smartest student would always go first. That was usually Pauline Tobias. I may have had a crush on her, too, but I know I always marveled at how she could read anything and seemed to know everything. She could read like a church elder. I'd wait around for the hands to thin out. Wait for the reading to get closer to the paragraph I'd memorized.

"Sister, sister, please, please call me," I'd plead. It usually worked. Passage read. My mind was now free to wander. There would be a price to pay later, of course, but why suffer today what could be put off until tomorrow. As long as no one found out, I thought I was safe. At the time the word *illiterate* wasn't known to me. I thought I was just stupid. Who could I tell? I adored my mother but couldn't disappoint her. My siblings already thought I was both spoiled and a geek. Better to find new ways to hide.

I felt out of place almost everywhere except in church. Church had always been my sanctuary, a place to escape the tension between my parents and forget about my own shortcomings. Through some combination of good fortune and

God's grace, I grew up in one of Baltimore's grand chapels. It was affectionately known on the black preacher circuit as the big house.

"We're marching to Zion! Beautiful, beautiful Zion! We're marching upward to Zion, the beautiful city of God!" That was the song that opened every Sunday service at New Shiloh Baptist Church. The old gothic building was originally built as a Lutheran church. In the age before mega-churches, New Shiloh was considered a big church in Baltimore. About a thousand people showed up for two Sunday morning services. A massive stained-glass window framed the pulpit. Scriptures etched in the high ceilings. And long wooden pews laced with soft cushions stood like soldiers in three rows, at least thirty rows deep. In the Baltimore of my childhood there were just a few certainties in every black neighborhood: a black-owned barbershop, beauty parlor, liquor store, funeral home, and the church.

For most of my childhood and adolescence, New Shiloh Baptist Church was the most sacred place on earth to me. I felt safe. I felt loved. I would have slept there if my mother had allowed it. No matter what had occurred in the days prior in the outside world, the songs, the prayers, the sermon, even the smell of the place, seemed to heal all that ailed me. The music spoke to me: "I'm sometimes up! I'm sometimes down! Almost leveled to the ground, but I'll keep on holding on!" Lots of people go to the beach for joy and peace, having the ocean waves wash over their toes and bodies. Who needed the sounds of the Pacific or the Atlantic? I had the New Shiloh Baptist Church mass choir and young adult choir twice on most Sundays.

My mom called church the poor man's therapy session. Ninety minutes of music and song and prayer and a sermon that sent you on your way encouraged and hopeful. There's no co-pay, just the offering plate. My childhood pastor once described church to me this way: "A warm spiritual bath."

New Shiloh was just one of a large number of churches sprinkled across the country with a reputation for drawing grand orators. Preaching at Shiloh was like playing at Carnegie Hall. Through the years, the voices of Reverends Martin Luther King Sr., Ralph Abernathy, and Andrew Young echoed in the sanctuary. The pastor, Reverend Harold A. Carter, a former associate minister to Martin Luther King Jr. in Alabama, was a preacher's preacher. He could hoot with the best of them. Sweat profusely on the coldest days. Draw out the name Jesus the length of the Great Wall of China. I could listen to that man read the words on a can of paint. Churches like New Shiloh have always taken great pride in honoring the oral history of the black church. There's great emphasis given to the spoken word. All my life I've known people who could quote the Bible but couldn't read it. Even in choir rehearsal, we learned most songs from a cassette recorder or at the director's instruction. "You can't learn the song by staring at paper," a choir director once told me. Amid all that joyous noise, it was seemingly a perfect hiding place for a poor reader.

Since no one in my family yet understood my inability to read, it didn't strike anyone as odd or alarming that I would volunteer to work for the radio ministry at church. Every Sunday night listeners could hear Reverend Dr. Harold A. Carter deliver one of his best Bible-thumping, scream-the-Scriptures, make-the-faithful-stand-up-and-shout kind of sermons. There was a small army of volunteers who served as engineers. During the morning service, one person a week would sit at the foot of the pulpit, a big bulky headset covering his ears and a reel-to-reel recorder the size of a suitcase at his fingertips, with several microphones strategically set up around the church. I wanted desperately to try; finally someone picked me. How hard could it be? I would soon find out.

After several weeks of training, I was set to record my first live Sunday morning service. The chief engineer promised he would be with me. That morning the phone rang. "Hey, Byron, I won't make it to church today. But you can do it. All the equipment's labeled. The instructions are all written out for you." A fire alarm should have gone off in my head. It didn't. I went to church figuring I'd memorized enough to get by.

The service was rocking. The spirit was high, and the choir sounded like angels from heaven. By accident I hit STOP on the recorder. The tape stopped. I panicked. I wasn't trained to cue up the tape and record again. Now sweating like the preacher winding down his sermon, I looked at the manual for direction. It might as well have been written in Braille. I couldn't read it. I couldn't fix the problem. And soon everyone would know I was stupid. For the remainder of the service I buried my head in my hands. Most people assumed I was praying. I wished I was dead. For the first time in my life, reading really meant something. And suddenly my safe place in church was no longer so safe.

That night my family gathered around the radio to listen to the service, but rather than Reverend Carter's rousing sermon from that morning, the city got to hear one of Reverend Carter's oldies-but-goodies. "What happened to today's ser-

vice?" my mother asked. "Must have been technical difficulty," I replied, with my chin buried in my chest.

"Hold your head up. I'm sure it'll be perfect next time,"
was my mother's response. There would be no next time. I
was never asked to record the service again, even though in
my aching heart I believed I could have gotten it right. And
I've never entered New Shiloh since without feeling the sting
of that day. My family assumed I got nervous or lost interest.
I knew better.

It was at about this age that I developed a reputation for
being quiet and sensitive. I would go almost an entire weekend without speaking. Easier still, I could avoid stuttering.
Little did I know then that a lot of children struggle with stuttering when they're first learning to speak. But from my childish perspective, I was simply a freak: The strange one, the one
who couldn't get the words out, couldn't do a simple thing
like speak clearly. For me, it was like living as a prisoner inside a cell. Oh, the things my heart wanted to say, the times I
wanted to yell at my parents to stop fighting, stand up to a
bully who taunted me, and the times I just wanted lemonade
in the school cafeteria but could only say the word *soda*. I've
never liked soda. Would never drink it if I had the choice. We
stutterers often think we have few choices in life, so during
my silent weekends I'd play baseball or football all day Saturday with my friends. Funny thing: I've never stuttered,
never felt out of place or insecure on any ball field. At the
time *self-esteem* was a term with little meaning in the world
of a child, but it's clear to me now I had very little self-esteem
back then. That may explain why harsh words from a teacher
would leave me in tears.

As frustrating as it was, my stuttering never kept me from singing. Like a lot of stutterers, my words flowed smoothly when accompanied by music. So I was excited to hear an announcement about a new community choir. Word went out at St. Katharine's elementary school that the archdiocese was putting together a mass choir for a highly publicized winter concert, and I wanted in. "Hey, Momma, can I join the Catholic chorus?" While school was rarely my favorite place, I loved to sing and loved being part of my church choir. I figured that enthusiasm would translate to this event. Since it was winter and I wasn't playing football, I knew I needed something to occupy my time and avoid schoolwork. Rehearsal was at St. Francis Catholic Church, a building just as old and just as breathtaking as my beloved New Shiloh. We rehearsed every Tuesday and Thursday night. Though I'd never become a radio engineer at church, I could stand in the back row of a choir and sing. That first rehearsal in the church basement was packed. Kids from at least a half dozen schools and several adults showed up. Many of them were really gifted singers.

I had wanted to participate because of my love for the New Shiloh Baptist Church choir. But the Catholic chorus was nothing like Shiloh. At Shiloh, rehearsal usually followed a routine: we would tell a few jokes, stand up and sing for about an hour, then pray and go home. Not the Catholic chorus. There were breathing exercises, stretching exercises, and vocal warmups. This wasn't choir rehearsal. This was boot camp.

At Shiloh, tenors stood in the back row. In this chorus, we were positioned by both size and section. God, why couldn't I be any taller? There I was, front row between a woman my grandmother's age and a teenage boy who sang like an angel and never once spoke to me. Maybe he knew I was stupid, not worthy of being acknowledged. And, oh yeah, we all had sheet music. This torture went on for weeks, and without a logical excuse it was too late to quit.

The choir director was a priest from Chicago who was as colorful as he was demanding.

"You can't sing pretty," the director announced. "Open your mouth wide! Enunciate! Sing UGLY, people! Articulate the words, people!"

I already thought I was odd and ugly without someone insisting I sing ugly. And to articulate words I could not read on paper was also a request beyond my abilities. Suddenly even one of my favorite activities, singing, was now threatened by demands I was unprepared to meet. My hiding places were disappearing. It was late February, the coldest days of winter, and my spirit was as chilled as the weather.

Despite the frigid temperature on the night of the performance, I couldn't stop sweating. And then there was the crowd. Not the familiar faces of my home church but hundreds of strangers. I just knew they were all looking and laughing at me. I was ten. I felt like one hundred.

"Good evening, ladies and gentlemen! Welcome," said the director.

Momma had bought me a new blue suit, white shirt, and brown shoes. Extra money spent, so this had to be a big occasion. My brother and I only got new suits for Easter. The shirt still had that new shirt stiffness. The shoes were still smooth at the bottom so I almost fell as we marched in. Each member of the chorus had a beautiful burgundy folder with our sheet music. It was useless to me. The church was full. People lined the walls. When the director cleared his throat, raised his hand, and cued the pianist, it was time. I was ready. Or so I thought. Through each anthem, hymn, and gospel tune, I mumbled or sang one word: *watermelon*. Whether we were singing at the top of our voices or in a whisper, slow cadence or at a deliberate pace, "watermelon, watermelon, watermelon" were the only lyrics to come out of my mouth, because someone in rehearsal had once told me, "If you're struggling with a song, just mouth the word *watermelon*."

That's what I sang for two hours. No one seemed to notice my strange enunciation, except Momma. I caught a glimpse of those piercing gray eyes. There was both displeasure and curiosity in those eyes.

"What were you doing?" she asked on the ride home. "It didn't look like you knew a single song," she said with disappointment. Once again, my poor performance was dismissed as nerves. But steadily the world was closing in.

The tension level around the house over my academic performance was starting to rise. I was a D student, struggling in a remedial reading class. I would bring home progress reports from school, hand them to my mother, and listen as she read them aloud. Unlike many of my friends, I never tried to steam open the notes from school before my mother read them. Why bother? The notes never made much sense to me anyway. One week, the note home was followed up with a phone call from school.

"Byron's failing math." The Ds were turning into Fs.

My mother had long believed any of life's difficulties could be wrestled to the ground with prayer, faith, humility, hard work, and the more than occasional use of harsh words. So Mom tried that same remedy for bad grades: "Got dammit, boy, you can do this!" That soon progressed to punishment. No television. No going outside, and sometimes I wasn't even allowed to go to choir rehearsal. It didn't make a difference. My math scores stayed rock bottom. Discussions at school were now about keeping me behind a year. And the biggest sin in my house—I was becoming a discipline problem. I never talked back to an adult, but I began to mouth off plenty with classmates. You see, around the playground, the word *stupid* was starting to follow my first name. Being polite and quiet was no longer enough to get by.

"Let's get Byron tested."

Despite the distractions of her own life, my mother was now fully engaged in finding out why I was struggling so with math. Could the school measure my capacity to do math? The archdiocese finally arranged to have me tested. The test took place somewhere in downtown Baltimore. My parents led me to believe we were going to a school. So why did it look like a hospital?

"Momma, are we in the right place?" I asked.

"Yes, honey!" Her answer lacked conviction. She put her hand at the nape of my neck as we walked up the stairs. The scene inside was no more reassuring. There were no children walking the halls. No artwork on the walls. It even smelled like a hospital. That wretched clean smell. As we sat in the waiting area, my father read a newspaper. My mother and I played that child's hand game. She always let met win. My small hands resting on top of her thick strong hands, but I had speed on my side.

"You're too good," she'd taunt me. For a moment I forgot where we were.

"Pitts family," yelled a man wearing a sports coat. He had a kind face. He ushered me into a room.

"Here's a pencil. Please take your time and answer each question."

The room resembled the set from the television show *Romper Room*. Nothing about it felt natural. I was a kid. I knew my way around a classroom. This place was foreign.

"Please focus and take your time" one of many gentle reminders from the man with the kind face. He sat behind a plain wooden desk, flipping pages on a clipboard and tapping a pencil holder crammed with pencils. I was through the test in twenty minutes, but it felt like two days. Some answers I thought I knew. Others I was not certain of, and the vast majority I simply made up. I treated much of the test like an art project. Coloring in the answer boxes in order to form a pattern on the page, instead of actually seeking the right answer to the question. When the test was over, I was sent back to the waiting area. My mom and dad were brought into a private room. Their discussion with some other adult seemed to go on much longer than the actual test. My father walked out first. He looked ashen and embarrassed. My mother looked as if someone had just punched her in the stomach.

"Son, let's go home." That's all she said. "We have to come back tomorrow for more tests." There was no further discussion that night. Two days out of school? I knew that wasn't a good sign.

That next day more tests and more closed-door meetings with my parents. Eventually we were all in the same room. Mom, Dad, me, and a woman they repeatedly referred to as Doctor. She was pleasant and spoke slowly and deliberately with a foreign accent. She asked me a series of questions.

"Do you like school? . . . Do you have many friends? . . . Do you get along with the members of your family?"

What's any of this have to do with math? I wondered. Then, to my parents' amazement, the therapist took a tape measure out of her pocket, leaned toward me, and measured my head. She wrapped the tape around my head as if she were sizing me up for a ball cap. She even touched my head just like my mother would touch melons at the grocery store.

My father yelled, "What the hell are you doing?"

With a straight face, the therapist asked my parents if I'd ever been tested for mental illness. My mother burst into tears. It was the first time I had ever seen my mother cry or even appear vulnerable in public. Mental illness? Does that mean I'm crazy? I'd never felt sadder. Why can't I hide? Why won't Momma stop crying? Why does Daddy look so angry? My father challenged the doctor's competence. Momma grabbed my hand, as if the room was on fire, and whisked me away with my father still yelling at the doctor. My head was throbbing, not from pain but from confusion. Wasn't this just a math test? Someone had neglected to tell my parents I'd failed every test they'd given me.

But that was the case: I'd failed so dramatically that there was concern my problems might go beyond reading and comprehension to mental illness. My parents were told that the archdiocese was going to seek funding to continue having me tested. And that's what happened. Weeks later we were sent to yet another testing facility for another tiresome day-long session, this time with psychologists and psychiatrists. I was interviewed by myself, with my mother, and separately with my father; then they were interviewed together. I was asked to draw pictures of my family. I drew a picture of my father in a suit and a picture of my mother as a queen with a halo. My picture of Saundra was of a teenager on a swing, and I depicted my older brother as a small man with no hands. It was left to the psychiatrists to figure out what all of the drawings meant. But they did conclude that I was not mentally ill. In fact, I demonstrated above-average intelligence.

They could not, however, answer the fundamental question of why I could not read. Their conclusion in a report to my parents: bring him back when he's thirteen. My mother's reaction: "Damn doc, we can't wait that long. He'll either be dead or in jail."

My parents took me home with overwhelming sadness and frustration and no more answers than when we started the testing process. My mother soon asked for a meeting at St. Katharine's and asked the teaching staff for some direction. In response, a staff member came to our house, bringing more test results and finally put a label on my problem. The diagnosis would set my young life on a new course.

The St. Katharine's staff member and I, along with my parents, were all sitting in our living room. He asked to speak to my parents privately, but Mother assured him that whatever he had to say was fine to say in front of me. He had actually brought the results of some tests my parents had not yet seen. His words will always ring in my ears.

"I'm sorry, Mr. and Mrs. Pitts. Byron is functionally illiterate."

My father frowned, my mother raised her hand to her mouth, and I looked puzzled. What does "functionally illiterate" mean? My parents were finding out that in all the years in school I hadn't learned to read. I'd faked and finagled. It wasn't that I couldn't do the math: I could not read the directions. All these years and no one had noticed. Sweet, polite, quiet Byron could not read. I could recognize some words, identify names of certain locations, remember the words I'd memorized at the kitchen table, the name of my school on the side of the building, and the names of my siblings attached to magnets on the refrigerator. I could function, but I could not read. My mother would say years later that it was one of the few nights she cried herself to sleep. Usually knowing is better than not knowing, but initial shock has a pain all its own. She's been asked on more than a few occasions, why didn't you know sooner that Byron couldn't read? The short answer: When did she have time? Two jobs, three kids, night school, and a cheating husband usually made for a very full day.

The anger and tension that often curled through our house like smoke up a chimney was suddenly replaced by sadness. Everyone felt it. Everyone dealt with it in different ways. My brother treated me like his best friend. My mother, whom I used to follow around the house, was now following me. This went on for weeks. As we searched for some resource, some long-term solution, my mother set out the short-term course.

"Okay, honey, if we've spent two hours on homework, we'll try four hours. We will pray when we start. We'll pray when we get tired. And we'll pray when we're done."

Just the idea of working longer hours seemed to make her happy. As sad as I was at the time, I remember the joy I felt in anticipating the journey. I had no control over how poorly I read at the time, but I did have control over how hard I worked. That's what you do if you're Clarice Pitts's child. You work hard.

"Smart people can think their troubles to the ground, honey," she'd say. "We have to wrestle ours."

Soon my father seemed disengaged from the process. He worked more overtime, or at least that's what he told my mother, and stayed away from the house for longer hours. I don't recall a single conversation we ever had after my diagnosis. Maybe he really was embarrassed. Relatives had long teased me, "You're a Momma's boy." From that moment and every day since, I've been proud to be a Momma's boy.

These were the darkest days of my life. It wasn't simply the shame of not knowing how to read: it was not knowing where to start. Unsure where the bottom was, it felt as if I was falling. My mother was holding my hand, but we were both just falling. How easy it would have been for her to give up. Give up on me, give up on her abilities or responsibilities as a parent. This was a vulnerable time for both of us. A working-class family, we lacked the resources to do much more than pray and look to others for help. There wasn't much help around, but the power of prayer was immeasurable. It created comfort where none existed. It revealed a path when earthly avenues seemed closed. And it provided strength that could be explained in no other way.

As my family prayed and looked for answers, a decision was made in school. I was removed from a regular classroom and placed in all remedial classes. I was about to spend fifth grade as one of "the basement boys." Smart kids were taught aboveground; children like me were sent to the basement.

When I had taken classes aboveground, there were those giant glass windows to look through to the street below. The kids in the basement looked up at a window and saw only the feet of people passing by. Deep in my heart, I knew I didn't belong there, or at the very least I had to escape. But I didn't know how. The classroom size was smaller, and these were kids with whom I had rarely spent time. Many often seemed angry, some were violent, and none seemed hopeful. In my regular class, my friends talked and dreamed of becoming teachers, doctors, lawyers, or sports stars. In my new class, the answer was almost always "I 'ont know." I don't know. It's the slogan for those without dreams or a path to follow.

For all the gloom of being a basement boy, this time also proved to be one of life's great teachable moments. I truly believe that it is possible to find good in every moment, especially the difficult ones. Until this point, my academic life was mostly one failure after another. Each day the new challenge had been to find a way to hide. Once I was assigned to the basement, the days of hiding were finally just about over. I can still remember the glance from classmates in the morning. The bright kids, or at the very least, the normal kids walked upstairs, and my kind headed to the basement. I could feel the looks of disdain at the back of my head. Worse still, I could sometimes hear the whispers of pity or contempt. "There go the dummies, fresh off the short bus."

No one at St. Katharine's in the late 1960s and early 1970s took the bus to school, but the reference to the short bus was a reference to kids with learning, physical, or emotional disabilities who went to special schools or were taught in different classrooms. I once overheard two adults in the basement chatting in the hallway. "Today the basement, tomorrow prison." It was clear the basement wasn't a place you went to learn. It's where you were warehoused until fate or the legal system had a place for you.

Many of those in the basement doubted their future, and so did many of those who were paid to be there to help us. Hopelessness breeds more hopelessness. It was the same for many of us in the basement. We tried covering up our academic deficiencies with attitude and bravado. At about five feet four and 90 pounds, thank God I was never able to pull off the tough guy act. My grandmother always said, "The good Lord gives us what we need." I guess He knew I needed to remain skinny and sheepish until He got me through middle school.

There was a whole new look, language, and protocol in the basement. The classrooms were mostly bare. Not a lot of decorative and inspirational learning tools attached to the walls. The desks were older. Supplies and books were more scarce. Basement teachers spoke harshly. Class often started with "Sit down and shut up!" Much more time was devoted to discipline than to education. Almost all of my classmates were boys. An early morning shoving match meant we might spend much of the day in silence in a darkened classroom. I saw the principal and other administrators many times in the hallways upstairs. The janitors' supply room was in the basement. Other than the teachers, the janitor was usually the only other adult down there. And there was a different approach to learning. We seemed to spend a great deal of time in group learning in the basement. We rarely had homework; assignments were completed in the classroom as a group. We still read aloud, but here the teacher would read first, then the entire class would repeat after her or him. Even blackboard assignments were done as a group. Upstairs, I always dreaded going to the blackboard alone, whether for math, reading, or history. Now we would go up two or three at a time.

Unlike many of my classmates, I still had an optimistic spirit. I still believed that, with hard work, success was possible. Upstairs, my optimism was met with skepticism and the clear sense I was naive or even stupid, but oddly, in the basement, at least some of my new friends welcomed me. Though shy and frequently bullied, I was mostly cheerful and could keep people entertained with humor or encouragement. As they did in sports, classmates often chose to work with me because I could make them laugh or lift their spirits. A favorite line from childhood on a ball field or in the classroom was always "We got this." In other words, we can win. Upstairs, I was always alone and afraid at the blackboard, but here I could be the encourager.

"If John went to the store with three dollars and bought

cereal for a dollar forty and gum for fifty cents, how much money would he have left?" the teacher would ask. We were to write out her question and answer it at the blackboard.

"We got this," I'd say through a ragged smile.

One boy would write; the other two would repeat the teacher's sentence and help with spelling. I treated those exercises like a sporting event. We were a team. The question was the opponent. It was easier to rally the group around a sports challenge than an academic problem. We often got the answer wrong, but I took joy in the effort. Upstairs, success was almost always measured by achievement (getting the right answer, passing the test), but here, at least in my heart, success could be measured by effort. No one can always know the right answer, but you can always give your best effort.

Those days in the basement were an early lesson on how to redefine success. Take life in small bites, until you can take on more. Find our own pace and stick to it. In a regular classroom, I was a kid on a tricycle trying to keep pace with cars on a highway. In the basement, some of us had tricycles and some had even less. Admittedly, I had one major advantage over most of my classmates. I had Clarice Pitts. Life has taught me there is a fast-moving river that separates success from failure. It's called giving up. Too many people drown in that river. As a boy in the basement, I was often caught in its undertow, but my mother was always nearby, screaming, encouraging, threatening, praying, and on occasion she'd even dive in to pull me out.

During my years in the basement at St. Katharine's, I always felt embarrassment entering and leaving the basement, but the feeling would subside once I was settled in my seat. I resigned myself to the idea that maybe it was where I needed to be for the moment. But it would not be my destiny—God had something greater in store. But, without question, this was the least optimistic time of my life. And my parents' fights were growing in frequency and intensity.

By sixth grade, I still hadn't learned to read well. And I was feeling a greater separation from the so-called normal world, wondering if I would ever return to it. Often alone at home, I had few reliable friends. They included Butch, the family dog; Wilson (long before Tom Hanks in *Castaway*), the name on my favorite football; and my constant after-school companion: television. Every weekday afternoon and as much of the evening as possible was spent watching television. It was my window to the world and a good escape from my troubles. One afternoon while watching *Captain 46*, the local cartoon show, I saw (and heard) an ad for a reading program for adults who couldn't read. I jotted down the number and told my mother. "Momma, if they can teach adults to read, then maybe it's not too late for me." We were both desperate by this time. She called the number and they agreed to try their program on me.

Days later, a man came to our house with a case that looked like it might have a small television set inside, which made me smile. But it wasn't a TV. It was a microfiche machine along with a box of slides. There was never any clear-cut diagnosis as to why I couldn't read, but we worked from the assumption that I missed the basics early on in grade school, fell behind, and either lost interest or couldn't keep up. The machine was meant to take me back to the beginning. Both my parents and my brother were trained in how to operate the equipment.

Every day after school and after finishing my homework, I was to spend at least one hour with my reading machine, going through the slides reflected on the TV-like screen. It was repetition, rote, memorization. The first lesson was on the alphabet. Learning to recognize and sound out letters. What I should have learned at age four, I was finally getting at age eleven. The session was occasionally interrupted by my uncontrollable tears. I cried in hysterics. "I'm almost in high school, and I'm studying the alphabet? I really am a moron. People will laugh at me. I'll never catch up."

My mother reassured me. "You're not a moron. Son, it doesn't matter how you start, only how you finish. You can do this. We can do this." So we did it, every single day, until the letters and then the words began to come more easily. I practiced until it became second nature.

One of the many great discoveries that came out of my illiteracy is the joy that can exist on the other side of heartache. It can be like the relief you feel after a good cry or the day after you get over the flu. It's often easier to appreciate good health in the immediate days after an illness. When the pain is gone. Such was the case months after I began working with the reading machine. As I've mentioned, until this point any notes from the teacher were delivered home unopened to my mother. The words on the paper read like Braille to me. I never waited around to see my mother's reaction because I could hear it soon enough. It was often "Byron! What the hell is this?" Rarely did teachers criticize my effort. It was always the outcome that fell short. But one day all that changed. Like a newborn to breast milk, I clung to my reading machine and quickly moved from the alphabet to simple sentences. Noun, verb, object. I was, in fact, reading. Well below grade average but reading nonetheless.

By the end of sixth grade there came another note from school. I remember running home with the note in my hand. The news was too big to fit in my bookbag. I bounced around the house like a ball in a pinball machine until my mother came home. In fact, I called to see if she could come home immediately.

"What's wrong, son, why should I come home early?" Years earlier I'd actually set the kitchen on fire. Something about experimenting with a toaster. Anyway, my pleas for her to come home early were always met with some apprehension after that.

"No, Momma, it's good news. Just get home early. I can't tell you over the phone."

"Okay, honey, I'll be there as soon as I can," she replied with an uneasy sigh.

Hours later I met her at the door. "I got a note from the teacher. Can I read it to you?" Those words had never come out of my mouth before. My eyes met my mother's. We were both smiling. I cleared my throat.

"Mrs. Pitts, Byron is doing better in school. He is showing real pro . . . pro . . . progress."

I looked up to see my mother with a big smile on her face and tears rolling down her cheeks. It would be the first and last time my mother and I cried together. They were tears of joy. Something so small remains one of the great highlights of my life. I believe she baked me a chocolate cake to celebrate.

Regardless of the obstacles in your way, one of the great wedges to get you past an obstacle is hard work. There's almost a renewable fuel you get from working hard. The harder you push, the further you realize you can go. As I see it, success is just your work made public. Through the years I've come to enjoy the hard work on the way to success more than the actual achievement. It's the joy of being in the midst of it. It's like a great glass of ice water. Water's good for the body almost any day, but after you've worked hard in the sun, is there anything better than a cold glass of ice water?

Hard work never lies. It may not always reward you in the ways and in the time you'd like, but it's always honest. When you've worked hard, you know where you stand. You know what you've given. I've always believed that someone else could outthink me or outmaneuver me, but I only feared the person who could outwork me. Fortunately, I haven't come across that person too often. It's actually a pretty small fraternity: hard workers. Look at almost any successful person in any field, and you'll find at least this one trait: an ability and willingness to work hard. It's the great equalizer. It's the one gift we can give to ourselves, too often overlooked as we "trade up" for a sexier approach. It's not a shortcut; rather, it's the straightest line to success. It's also a great building block for acquiring other important life skills.

Every door that's ever opened for me in life started by my knocking hard and sometimes even kicking, putting my shoulder against it, and if not patiently, then prayerfully, waiting for it to open or fall off its hinges. Even as a kid who couldn't read, I knew I was fortunate. I had the gift. I knew how to work hard because my mother taught me.

And so it began. The first steps to overcoming my childhood shame of illiteracy. Pure, raw, uncomplicated hard work. Except for a few school administrators and teachers, no one outside my immediate family ever knew I couldn't read. Most days I was deathly afraid of failure, but I refused to let the outside world see it. The mask was coming off . . . but ever so slowly.

Years after that horrible day in the doctor's office, I can still remember my mother's words as we walked to her car: "Keep your head up, son. When we get home, we'll pray about it. Work our way through it." She rubbed the top of my head, pulled at my chin, and then took my hand. I've never walked with my head down since that day.

THREE

Quiet Discipline

And say unto him, Take heed, and be quiet; fear not, neither be fainthearted. . . .

—Isaiah 7:4

SUMMER WAS ALWAYS A welcome relief from the stress and strain of my school life. And summers meant time with my grandma, Roberta Mae Walden. If it was my mother who taught me the power of passion, it was my mother's mother who taught me the strength that exists in calmness. For my mother it was discipline by force, but for my grandma it was quiet discipline. Both had the same goal: to be tough enough to survive any obstacle. But my grandmother wasn't much of a talker. She was a doer. She'd show her love by making your favorite dessert from scratch. Each grandchild had a favorite. Mine was her chocolate cake with buttermilk. She wouldn't say she loved you very often. She'd always just show you with a hug, a smile, or a laugh at a grandchild's lame jokes. She wasn't big on lecturing, and I never heard her raise her voice. I learned by her example.

As a boy, I spent most summers in Apex, North Carolina. My parents would always drop me off at the end of the school year. After an eight-hour drive from Baltimore, with R&B music and a bucket of Kentucky Fried Chicken in the car, they'd stay a day or two and then head back north. Grandma's home address said Apex, but she lived in the community of Friendship, a spit of a town with two churches, no more than five hundred houses, and not a single traffic light. The Friendship of my youth was a place of dirt roads, open overgrown fields, and weekend barbecues after the local adult league baseball game. Tobacco was still king. Eventually, the tobacco fields would be replaced by subdivisions. So today the sweat-stained overalls of tobacco growers and vegetable farmers have been replaced by salivating developers in khaki pants and blue blazers. Raleigh is twelve miles from Friendship, and as the state capital has spread its boundaries, with Northerners and people from other parts of the country pouring into the South, towns like Apex and Friendship have blossomed into bedroom communities.

In the 1960s my grandmother owned about thirty acres of wooded property. It remains a place where the air is clean and where deer, rabbits, and all kinds of creatures have always found a safe watering hole. There was a shed out back that contained all of her yard tools, including a saw and an ax. It might seem like a dangerous space for a small child, but no one ever worried about the grandkids playing in that shed because it was also a favorite resting place for snakes. My earliest memories include the outhouse and a deep well with one single metal bucket, a chain, and a hook. It was almost too heavy for me to carry, but I would slosh water, along with a cousin, into the house a few times a week.

Every summer vacation would begin the same way. I'd walk through the door of her shotgun house, and she'd greet me with a broad smile, a strong hug, a kiss on the cheek, and the same words in a whisper: "You're the one." Each night as she sent me off to bed, another hug and kiss and those same words uttered in a whisper: "You're the one."

Honestly, I never really knew what she meant. Just that I never wanted to let her down. And no matter what I thought of myself and my shortcomings, this old woman, with thinning hair, penciled-in eyebrows, and one crooked finger, believed in me and loved me unconditionally.

With my parents back in Baltimore, summers at my grandmother's house meant freedom. Cousins lived in nearly every other house. My grandmother, her sister, and her brother had married two brothers and one sister from the same family, so almost everyone in Friendship was (and is) either a Walden or a Womble. I spent my days eating Grandma's home cooking, kicking stones down dusty country roads, playing pickup baseball games, chasing skinny dogs, catching black snakes, spying on giant black ants, and washing down the day's adventures with a moonpie and a sweet tea. North Carolina may be the Tar Heel state, but for many of us who love it, it's also the pork barbecue and sweet tea capital of the universe. It's a place where locals eat hush puppies and most everyone has a nickname. In my family there's a Preacher, an uncle named Feel, a Piggly Wiggly, a Honey Bun, a Chief, a Señorita, Sonny, Hambone, and Poss . . . the short version of my mother's childhood nickname, Possum. There is a story behind every one, and each nickname was meant as a term of endearment. At the center of it all was Momma, as all her children and grandchildren called her. She was Señorita to her closest friends and Miss Roberta to the rest of the world. Her mother, my great grandmother, was born a slave. But there was nothing remotely subservient about Miss Roberta.

Looking back, I realize that one of the reasons I loved those summers in Apex so much was that all the fears of my life washed away. It was a simple existence, not complicated by the subterfuge it took to get homework done or the torment of feeling like the stupid kid in the neighborhood. Friendship was a great place to hide out for a kid who couldn't read or speak clearly. My aunts, uncles, cousins, and my grandmother's friends would always say, "Byron is such a good boy. He's so quiet and polite." My grandmother's long-time boyfriend would always add, "You give that boy a glass of milk and a TV, you'd never know he was in the house." That was high praise for a kid in my position.

I never did a stitch of homework in Apex, but I gained an invaluable education. It was a lesson taught without books or pencils or pens but with a stare, a raised finger, or a simple instruction. My grandmother wanted me to learn that an adversary can be beaten without harsh words or raised fists. That fear can be overcome with a calm resolve. That even an enemy can be treated with respect. It was her lesson in quiet discipline, and it all started with my insatiable sweet tooth.

A Zero candy bar was like a Milky Way bar, except it was white chocolate on the outside. It looked funny, but it was the best thing I had ever tasted. I don't even know if they make them anymore, but at age seven it was my absolute favorite. For some reason, I ate them only when I went to North Carolina in the summer to visit my grandmother. Never even looked for them in Baltimore. (Side note: after someone told me I was a Zero just like that candy bar, I stopped eating them altogether.) My burning desire for a Zero led me to a neighborhood grocery store one summer's day and, ultimately, the wrath of my grandmother.

In those days there were two stores within a mile of my grandmother's house. Segregated stores. My grandmother had brought me with her to do some shopping at the colored store. It was about the size of a trailer, with a dusty hardwood floor and a musty smell. It housed a big red cooler with a Pepsi Cola sign, lots of what I called "man" cigarettes (Kools and Marlboros), smoked meats, and the BC Powder that the women in the family used to treat all their pain, from monthly cramps to migraines. I loved to hear the musical tones of the manual cash register when the numbers would pop up and the drawer would close. My grandmother was taking her time, mulling over the fruit and vegetable stands out front and socializing with her friends. I was seven years old, and I had enough money in my pocket to buy a grape soda, a Zero candy bar, and a moonpie, and to have some change left over. But this store didn't have a Zero. So, without asking my grandmother, I wandered out the door and across the street to what looked to me like a better option.

The whites-only grocery store was fully stocked, refrigerated, and so well lit that from a distance I could see a box of Zeros just fingertips away from the cash register and a few inches away from the man at the register. He was big and a sunburned reddish color, wearing overalls, and I could smell an odor of chewing tobacco. There were other men and a few women in the store, but it was his stare that locked on me as I walked toward the front counter.

I was steps away from my precious Zero candy bar, and not aware of how much trouble I was in until I turned around and my eyes met my grandmother's eyes as she stood in the doorway. She hadn't even said my name, but somehow I had known she was there. She was afraid to walk in. But she knew she had to get me out, with her brand of quiet discipline. She didn't make a sound. In fact, she looked at me and smiled. The urgency was in her eyes. She tilted her chin down, raised one hand toward the middle of her chest, and with that arthritic finger twisted by age and hard work, she gestured for me to walk toward her. She didn't blink. She didn't glance away, and she kept that smile on her face. I turned my shoes in the opposite direction and moved toward her with my arms hanging at my sides.

Before I could reach her, the store clerk shouted, "Miss Roberta, what you doing here?"

"Just tending to my grandson," she said. "We'll be on our way." Her tone was gentle yet firm. Her voice did not betray her, and she never took her eyes off me. I left without my Zero candy bar. As we walked briskly to her car, she squeezed my hand tighter than she ever had before. "We'll talk in the car," she said under her breath.

My grandmother had never spanked me, but that day she came close. I was snuggled next to her in her old Chevy, and my grandmother said, "Don't you ever scare me like that again. There are people in this world who will hurt you just because of the color of your skin. So always be careful. Never be afraid or at least never show it. God won't call you home till your time. But in case He's not watching, you guard yourself." Then she smiled. It was a crash course in how to maneuver in the midst of segregation. We would not discuss it again until I was almost an adult. Then she told me, "I wasn't sure if I should scream or cry first. I didn't think anyone would hurt you, but in those times most anything was possible."

I never wandered in that store again either. Well after segregation ended, I still refused to go in. Fortunately, it was one of the few reminders in my life of what America was and how far we've come.

Whether it's a segregated grocery store or a schoolyard bully, I've remembered the lesson my grandmother taught me that day: Always know where you are and always carry yourself appropriately and respectfully. She wanted me to know that if I was afraid, it should never overwhelm me, and if I was angered by ignorance, I could remain calm and not confrontational. Because I was better than that. But it's one thing to know the lesson. It's another to live it, especially when she wasn't there to hold my hand on the playground or the street back in Baltimore, where I was often afraid for one reason or another. It was the fear of being exposed. The gnawing fear of not being good enough. Fear that my parents' angry words would lead to a split in my family. The fear of letting people down. The truth is, I didn't want to learn to read so that I could actually read. I wanted to learn to read so my mother wouldn't be ashamed, and I wanted to learn to read so people would stop making fun of me.

Small in stature, I was a frequent target of bullies, and the experience has haunted me for decades. Yes, I said decades. I've had nightmares about things I experienced as a child. I've awakened to night sweats and a clenched fist, angry and afraid. They'd take my lunch money and any shred of confidence I might have had. Simple things like going to the bathroom during school horrified me. Alone in the boys' room, kids like me were frequently targeted by bullies. Eventually, even my siblings became my tormentors. Our conversations would usually end with me crying and running to my mother. It became an endless cycle.

There was the group of boys who regularly chased me home from school calling me a sissy. I told my mother I didn't want to go to school anymore because I was afraid. (Actually, it was just another on a growing list of reasons why I didn't want to go.) Her solution was to have my older brother leave his friends and serve as my bodyguard. No wonder he hated me until we were in our twenties.

Then there was the sandwich-stealer. I never knew his name, his age, or where he went to school or lived. But he's lived inside my head since grade school. As best I can recall, we had one encounter. It was rare in our family that there was ever enough extra money around for things like lunch, beyond what was provided in the cafeteria or inside my metal lunch pail. I almost always took a bologna sandwich on white bread with mustard, a piece of fruit, and a Thermos filled with my favorite flavored Kool-Aid. Perhaps once or twice a year, my mom would give me lunch money to eat off-campus with my classmates. What a treat. A chance to buy my own food. It was one of life's simple pleasures that came to an abrupt end.

With three dollars in my pocket and a smile on my face, I walked out of St. Katharine's elementary school, crossed the street, and walked the half block with a few of my classmates to the corner sub shop. The sub shops and Chinese restaurants in the Baltimore of my youth all pretty much looked the same. They had high counters, bulletproof glass, and a menu written out by hand near the ceiling. I would later learn that the high counter and bulletproof glass were meant to discourage thieves. It would be hard to stick-up a sub shop or Chinese restaurant if you had to hold the gun above your head and stand on your tiptoes to threaten the clerk. There were no such safety measures for customers.

From early that morning, when my mom gave me money for lunch, I rehearsed over and over again what I would order. There was no chance I'd try and order off the menu. Someone might detect I could not read it, so I would order what I always ordered when I'd been in a sub shop with my family: a cheeseburger with lettuce, tomato, onions, with hot peppers. All morning in class my mind wandered to that moment. I watched the clock and could almost hear the seconds tick away. Finally the moment had come. I tilted my head up to see the clerk as I gave my order. No worries about reading the menu or stuttering. I'd practiced every word. I was ready. The sandwich was a dollar and seventy-five cents, one small order of fries for seventy-five cents, and one grape soda for a quarter. I was set. The smell of French fries and onions frying, the sizzle of a beef patty on the grill—it was all so intoxicating. My friends all ordered their favorites, from pizza slices to chicken parmesan and steak sub sandwiches. We were happy and laughing as we headed back to school. No one seemed to notice the teenager standing just outside the door. Who was he? Why wasn't he in school? All questions I would ask myself later, and over and over again for years.

"What's in the bags?" he asked.

My friends took one look, heard a threat, and ran. I was still trying to figure out why this big kid wasn't in school. With my friends gone, there we stood. This jerk didn't know my story. Didn't know I couldn't read or that I lived inside my shell. But he could apparently smell something on me besides a free meal. Pickle Pitts and this boy at least three years older and a good bit larger. He was smiling: not a friendly smile but as menacing as you could imagine. It was at that moment I caught a glimpse of his gold tooth. A gold tooth was a popular symbol of something back in the late 1960s and early 1970s. Symbol of what I was never certain. A plain gold tooth or one with a diamond shape in the middle or a champagne glass. Weird, I know. This guy had a champagne glass in his. He smelled like cigarettes.

"What's in the damn bag?" he growled. The smile was gone.

"My lunch," I answered.

"No, bitch, that's my lunch." That sickening smile was back.

I was frozen, gripped by fear and anger and shame. I couldn't move my legs. He grabbed for the bag, but I wouldn't let it go. It was a tug of war over my lunch and my boyish manhood. The bag ripped, the French fries scattered across the cement. The cheeseburger wrapped in aluminum foil rolled on the ground. My eyes welled up with tears. The French fries were wasted, and so was my mother's hard-earned money. This bully with thick stumpy arms bent over and picked up the sandwich, unwrapped it and took a bite. I watched as the gold tooth pierced the bun, his mouth covered with mustard and mayonnaise. Without knowing it, I guess my eyes narrowed and I clenched my fist.

"Oh, sissy boy wants to fight?" the bully asked in a mocking tone. He took his free hand and pushed my face.

"Get out of here before I hurt you." Then he kicked at me and pushed me away.

I stumbled, regained my footing, and backpedaled a few steps.

Why won't you fight back? I asked myself. Not only was I a moron; now I was a coward. My parents' money and I was too much of a coward to fight for it! Worse than losing a few dollars, it was the loss of dignity and self-respect that were most costly. I walked back to school in a daze, my eyes still burning, my head down. My pockets and my stomach were empty.

My classmates were waiting in front of the school. "What happened? Why didn't you run with us?" they asked.

I never opened my mouth. Like that moment in the car with my parents, outside my father's girlfriend's house, there were no words. My expression was blank. I shut down. The bell sounded and we proceeded back to class. From my desk I could look out the window and see the corner of the sub shop. The bastard who took my food was still standing there. I knew he couldn't see me, but I've always thought he was staring and laughing at me. I've had nightmares about him. That evening when my mom asked me to tell her about the events of my day, I never mentioned the incident. It still causes a pang of anger and shame. It's probably one reason I have such contempt to this day for bullies. I can still remember what that bully looks like. How much I wanted that cheeseburger. The sense of violation. Eventually, I would learn to stop being a victim. It was an important step on my journey. I have always used my grandmother's tactic of quiet discipline. I do not shout. I do not curse. I do not show fear. But I guard myself with self-respect against the bullies of the world.

On days of victory and days of defeat, my grandmother's words have always brought me great comfort. A peace. A reason to believe I never had to be the victim. My faith teaches me that there are no mistakes in life, just opportunities to learn.

FOUR

Who's Got Your Back?

For twenty years the old man went outside every day and a dug a hole looking for gold. Each morning he'd look out his window, and as far as he could see, there were holes in the ground. One moment he'd smile because those holes were testimony to his discipline. And the next moment he'd frown because he could hear voices laughing from deep inside the holes: What a fool he'd been, wasting his life digging holes looking for gold! Finally, the day came when he stopped digging and just stayed home. The next day he heard a great commotion coming from the center of town. He went to investigate. And there to his great disappointment was a young man with a chest full of gold. He told the masses gathered around him that he followed a trail of holes that went on for as far as the eye could see. Right where the holes stopped, he decided to dig. He found a chest full of gold. Now he was rich. All his dreams would come true.

If I had a piece of gold for every time Clarice Pitts told that story, I would be a rich man. It was her favorite story when she wanted to make a point about the value of staying on course. We are all reminded at times in our lives, how difficult it is to stay on course. Getting off course is a four-letter word: *easy.* Lord knows, at different moments, easy is fun, exciting, and even a bit dangerous. I learned at an early age that staying on course requires a long line of people, like a team sport. But sometimes, I discovered, I had to be at the front of the line and play the game alone.

"The first team to ten wins." That was the one basic rule to street basketball in my neighborhood. Fouling was encouraged, but complaining about a foul was not. Timmy Johnson was the best athlete around. Given the choice, every kid wanted to be on Timmy's team. Not only was he gifted, he was gracious. He might score 9 of 10 points, but he always shared the credit with his teammates. It was a Saturday night, and luck was on my side. Timmy picked me for his team, and we were up, 8–5. There was plenty of time to finish off our opponent and get home before dark. One of Clarice's many rules, "Be home before dark or else." Rarely did any child in our family dare test "or else."

While I was imagining my mother's delight when I walked in the door before she had to yell *BYYYY-RUUUN!*— the kid guarding me stole the ball. Suddenly it was 8–6, then 8–7, and a moment later, 8–8. How awful. We were now in a tight game. Worse still, there was a chance I might not make it home before dark. Damn. Thank goodness Timmy Johnson had a jump shot. We won 10–8. No time for the customary hand slap and trash talk. I had to run. And run I did for about three blocks. It was already dark, so no chance I'd make it. Momma would be waiting, and she'd be angry. What was my excuse? Didn't have one. So run faster. I cut across Mr. Frog's yard (you never walk on anyone's grass, but this was an emergency), jumped over the bush on the right corner of our porch, and slid all the way to the front door.

"Okay. Catch your breath, walk in quietly," I whispered to myself. What did it matter? My mother could be in a room without windows, and she'd still know when the sun went down. It must be some microchip God places in all good mothers. What excuse could I use? That wouldn't matter. It was dark and that meant "or else." Well, at least we won the game. Going to bed early ain't so bad. Getting a whooping, how long could that last? I was resigned to my fate, when much to my surprise, I entered the house and my mother was *not* waiting. Instead, I could hear her and my father arguing in their room. Profanity and anger. First, I felt great relief. Then I was overcome by a sense of loneliness. My parents had no idea whether I was at home or in the street. There was no "or else." I listened to them fight for quite a while, and then I surprised myself. I went back outside and down the street. Slowly at first, assuming my mother would notice my absence and yell for me to come back. She never did. And soon I was beyond earshot or sight of home.

I'd never been out past dark. The street looked different. People I'd never seen before were on the street. My friends were the jock crowd. All we needed was daylight and a ball. But Timmy Johnson was nowhere in sight. These people were standing around. Men and a few women with bottles, beer cans, and bad attitudes inhabited the basketball court. "Hey, shorty, what are you doing?" Who was this stranger speaking to me? "Come here for a second. Come do me a favor." Too scared to run, I walked closer. The guy reached in a pocket. Is this how my life ends? Boy shot, stabbed, hit in the head with a blackjack? My imagination had gotten the best of me. "Shorty, go to the store for me." He'd pulled out a roll of cash thick as his fist. "So-so-so-sorry, sir. I sh-sh-sh-should be-be-be home."

"What! Talk like you got some sense. You stupid or something?" I couldn't move. I couldn't speak. And I was angry. How dare this fool with liquor on his breath insult me?

He and his group laughed and turned back to their conversation. It was clear, at that moment, that this man was no better than I and I no better than he. He was, however, a cautionary tale. His world was not my world. Even as a boy, it was clear to me what his tomorrows might hold for him.

As for me, I returned home. I presumed my parents were still yelling, no one would be looking for me, but I at least had the choice of returning to my home. When I got to Federal Street, my parents were now silent and segregated in different parts of the house. That night, no one noticed I'd just come home after 10:00 P.M. I was a boy, but I felt like a thirty-year-old man. I'd just learned I was as much responsible for my own well-being as the adults in my life. I had to watch my own back.

It's one of the phrases you hear growing up in an urban

environment. Almost every city kid from eighteen to eighty-one has either used it or heard it: "Who's got your back?" It's part of the free education on the street, for which Ivy League schools require large sums of money. In a lot of ways, my neighborhood was just like corporate America. Take, for example, what the business world calls networking. You can't move up in a corporation without a network of mentors and supporters. In the world of my youth, these were called Homeys or Uncle So and So or Auntie So and So. (The key is to make sure the people who've got your back are positive role models and not losers.)

Who had my back when I was growing up? Like any kid who loved sports, I adored my coaches, and they looked after me. There was George Cook, my first Pee Wee football coach. Mr. Cook worked a part-time job with my father and loved teaching kids the fine art of tackling and blocking. At first glance, this small knotty man of Irish German descent, who did shift work at Bethlehem Steel and tossed back Budweiser with his buddies at a watering hole in East Point, Maryland, would seem to have very little in common with a black kid from East Baltimore. Mr. Cook was my first hero who didn't look like me. He was also a testament to something my mother always said: "Everyone your color is not your kind. There are some good white folk in this world."

For four seasons (1969 to 1972), Mr. Cook helped shuttle me back and forth from home to football practice and games, and we got to know each other pretty well. I'm certain he never knew my struggles with literacy, but I'm convinced that if he had, he would have done his level best to help. For all that escaped me in the form of words, much of my early learning came in examples shown by people like Mr. Cook who set an example with actions and his words.

"Pitts, you like tacos?" Mr. Cook asked me once. He'd stuffed me and several of my teammates in his car after a game and wanted to treat us after a win.

"What's a taco?" I asked him. At this point, my taste didn't go much beyond my parent's home cooking and an occasional cheeseburger. My teammates (all white) got a big laugh out of my ignorance.

"Shut up laughing," Mr. Cook barked. "There's no shame in asking what you don't know, son."

Coach Cook, besides my mother, was the first adult who encouraged me to push beyond familiar boundaries. It was enough that he took interest in ways my father never did or for which my father could never make time. In fact, it was during my last Pee Wee football season that my parents' marriage finally came to a merciful end. As my father would explain several years later, "We grew apart. Clarice was no longer the woman I fell in love with."

That statement is absolutely true. William Pitts was a full-time meat cutter and a part-time cab driver on the day he met my mother. He was a full-time meat cutter and a part-time cab driver on the day they separated. Clarice was a girl from the country with a tenth-grade education on their wedding day. When the marriage ended, she was a college graduate with a degree in sociology and a respected social worker, mostly helping single mothers find their way. My parents had indeed grown their separate ways. While William ultimately walked away from both his marriage and his children, Clarice swore, "When I leave, everything that eats goes with me." That meant her stepson, Mac (my sister was away at college), me, and Butch, the mangy dog a stranger left in my father's cab one night.

Clarice left William on Christmas Eve morning in 1972. He left for work and before his key could hit the ignition, his wife was up peeping through the curtains. When his car rounded the corner, she woke all of us up and called her brother. "He's gone. Let's go." By sunset we had a new address, 4817 Truesdale Lane.

While the marriage was falling apart, there were no funds or inclination for babysitters, so I usually tagged along most places my mother would go: church, occasionally to work, night school, even bars. "Anywhere I can go, my children can go" was her motto. I met some really neat people playing Foosball and drinking a grape soda while my mother sat at the bar and had drinks with her friends. That's also how I first met James Mack, barking instructions at my mother and others taking a swimming class at the Morgan State College swimming pool. He seemed rather impatient at the time. "I hope you people study better than you swim," he crowed.

"What are you doing in my class" he snapped at me as I sat in the bleachers.

"Sir," was my sheepish response. With a stern look, he approached me.

"Why are you sitting in my class? You a freshman?"

"No, sir" was my only response.

The frown melted from his face, and with a smile he said, "You look like a freshman. What's your name, champ?"

"My name is By . . . By . . . By . . . ron Pitts, sir. My mu . . . mu . . . mother is in your class."

"Clarice Pitts is your mother? I hope she's a better mother than she is a swimmer." With that, he laughed and returned to yelling at his class.

James Mack coached the men's swim team at Morgan State in the 1970s, as well as a recreational league wrestling team (so everyone called him Coach). By coincidence, he was also a revered deacon and taught Sunday school at my New Shiloh Baptist Church. There were deacons at church who could bring the congregation to tears and shouting. They spoke with such clarity and force it seemed even God would have to stop what He was doing and listen to their prayers.

For all his talents, praying was not Mr. Mack's gift. I never saw a grown man so nervous or sweat so much in church as the rare occasion when Mr. Mack was called to pray. Once he got past "Dear Heavenly Father . . ." it was often downhill. But ask any young man whose life was touched by Mr. Mack, and you would know God uses all kinds of folks in many ways. There were countless boys, myself included, who wished we had a father like Coach Mack. Perhaps because he only had daughters, he was more than willing to step in when he saw a boy who needed a man's influence.

Coach was a bulldog on stilts: a thick jawbone connected to a barrel chest stopping at the waist. If Coach weighed 200 pounds, he was 190 from the waist up, atop 10 pounds of bowlegged twisted steel. The only thing funnier than watching Coach Mack pray was watching him teach swim class in trunks and flip-flops (Adonis he was not). He always addressed me and every other kid as champ. ("Either you're a champ or a chump, and you look like a champ to me," he'd say.) He quickly joined the short list of adults I lived to please.

I don't believe in luck or chance. It was God's grace that brought Coach Mack into my life. I would never be the same. Over the years, Coach taught me to believe that there are no quick fixes. "Lottery tickets are for people looking for shortcuts," he would say. "Shortcuts are for cowards. Cowards don't know God." To this day I have never purchased a lottery ticket, to honor the sentiments of Coach Mack. Success, he often reminded me, was an investment. That's what I loved about Coach Mack. Big lessons in short definitive sentences. I'm sure he was wrong plenty of times, but he was never in doubt. There are probably dozens of cops, lawyers, teachers, counselors, probation officers, coaches, and at least one journalist from East Baltimore now living across the country who owe many of their core values and beliefs to Coach Mack. He helped to keep us all on the right side of trouble. In the neighborhood where I grew up, there was a line that must never be crossed. On one side was education and opportunity, on the other side was incarceration. It was all too easy to cross that line. It was why my mother fought so hard, and what Coach Mack understood so well. One misstep could change the course of a life forever. Coach Mack almost certainly changed that course one day when I was walking to school.

"Hey, champ, what's in the bag?" The night before, I had purchased a pocketknife from the corner store and was on my way to school the next morning when I bumped into Coach Mack. He's never told me how he knew, or maybe it was fate, but this was the one and only time I ever ran into Coach

Mack on my way to school and he asked to see inside my book-bag. Respectfully, I pulled out my books, my lunch, my pencils, even the bubble gum I'd planned on chewing later.

"Anything else," he asked. No, sir! I obviously answered too quickly.

"You sure?"

Perhaps it was the perspiration that gave me away? "Just this." I raised the pocketknife to Coach, as if it was an eighty-pound bag of shame.

"What's the knife for?"

Using the best reasoning available to an eleven-year-old on short notice, I explained to Coach that there was a bully at school who had tormented me for weeks. He'd taken my lunch, and on those rare occasions I had lunch money, he'd taken that too. Since I felt I had no options, the pocketknife would be the equalizer.

"So are you going to stab him or just scare him?" Coach asked. Coach was a real man. He understood my dilemma instinctively.

"Only if I have to, Coach."

"Why don't you practice on me?"

"No sir, Coach. I love you like a father."

"Son, it's not about loving me. It's about loving yourself enough not to do something you know in your heart is wrong." He did not ask. I handed him that brand-new knife. As best I know, he never told my mother and we never discussed it again.

"Love yourself enough," he said. No one had ever told me that before. No one needed to tell me again. Once from Coach was enough.

I shudder to think where I might be without Coach Mack's intervention. Where that knife might have landed, and landed me. He continued to be a part of my life well past college. He supported me in any way he could. Pocket money, on occasion, when I had a date. A sounding board on those frequent occasions my mother's strict rules were enough to drive an adolescent crazy.

What motivates men like Coach Mack? Where does that desire to help come from? I never had the chance to ask him. The last time I saw him at a college basketball tournament, he was in the early stages of Alzheimer's disease, and he barely recognized me. The man who'd guided so many young boys to manhood was now being escorted around by a group of men, some his contemporaries and a few of them guys my age who likely have their own Coach Mack stories. The things he had taught me, all he meant to me, were my memories alone. That same smile was there, but this time it was me saying, "Hey, Champ, good to see you."

At this point in my early teens, most of those watching my back had come from the ranks of my family, my parents' friends, or my community. And with the exception of Coach Cook, they had all been African American, like me. But a culture shock awaited me when I stepped through the doors of my new high school in September of 1974.

Baltimore's Archbishop Curley High School is where blue-collar kids could dream white-collar dreams, as a teacher once described my alma mater. Founded in 1962, it was one of the last all-boys Catholic high schools built in Baltimore, a modest three-story brick building run by Franciscan priests. Their parsonage was attached to one end of the building, next to the school chapel. The population was more than nine hundred boys, most of them Catholic, all but four of them white. So being black and Baptist made me stand out. It was a place that valued discipline, education, service, and physical fitness equally. Curley was, among other things, a jock school. We won championships in football, soccer, cross country, basketball, wrestling, baseball, lacrosse, and track. There was a dean of discipline, Mr. Murphy. His sole purpose in life, it seemed, was to scare teenage boys straight. It was a badge of honor to graduate from Curley without a single scare from Mr. Murphy.

There were a handful of lay teachers, but mostly there were Franciscans in their black robes, dark shoes or sandals, with a white rope around their waist. The three knots in the rope symbolized their vows of poverty, chastity, and obedience. Just seeing those men each day in their black robes with the three white knots changed my perspective on life. Till this time I'd seen sacrifice only as one of the shackles of a modest upbringing. People did without because they had to. But these Franciscans did without by choice, a commitment to service to others. I found the whole concept liberating. It lifted a burden I often felt as the son of a single parent, who was forced to sacrifice so much in order to provide for her children. Now I saw nobility in sacrifice. At the same time, their lifestyle fit perfectly with my mother's notion of hard work or building toward some greater goal. These men were sacrificing to serve God, and their reward would come in heaven. Perhaps if I sacrificed the sinful lures of adolescent life, like drugs and alcohol, then my reward would also come later. So, every day as I walked down the hallway, that concept beat in my brain and heart like a drum. Sacrifice was good. Sacrifice was honorable. I was no longer some poor kid with problems trying to do better. I was a child of God sacrificing now for rewards later, hopefully long before heaven.

By the time I got to Curley, I was no longer functionally illiterate, but I still read well below grade level and was placed in a remedial reading class. Based purely on grades, I probably shouldn't have even gotten into Curley. My admission was more a testament to the power of prayer and the force of my mother's personality. For years teachers talked about my admissions interview. Not about *my* interview but about *my mother's* interview. She pleaded, cajoled, and convinced. Thank God. I've often said those were the four best years of my life. I've never learned, laughed, or cried more in any four-year stretch since. Oddly enough, many people in my life thought Curley was a bad idea. A number of my mother's friends, and even a few relatives, questioned the environment and the expense. (Tuition was nine hundred dollars per year, a steep sum on a social worker's modest salary.)

"Why you send Byron to school with those white people?" one co-worker asked her.

Her answer was always the same. "When it comes to my children, I don't have to justify my actions to anyone. I will do what I think is best for them, *period*." There was rarely any follow-up comment.

She did explain her reasoning to me. "You need to see how white people think and work if you're going to work and succeed in a predominantly white world." That's why Clarice sent me to Curley. "I want you to get the best education available, and Curley is a good school. Plus, they will whoop your ass as quickly as I will if you get out of line." Regardless of the situation, discipline was never far from Clarice Pitts's mind.

My first real teachable moment at Curley had nothing to do with the classroom. And the first ass whooping did not come from a teacher. In 1974, America's racial divide seemed far away from Archbishop Curley. I was never targeted because of my color, though on one occasion it was as good a reason as any for a group of upperclassmen to push me around. The first week of high school I spoke to no one and no one spoke to me. I walked to school alone. It was about a two-mile walk through my racially mixed neighborhood, past a predominantly black housing project, a white blue-collar neighborhood, and finally the homestretch through the school parking lot, which had its own diverse hood: some obnoxious upperclassmen who had cars and angry boys who didn't have cars. Needless to say, I always viewed the school parking lot and the housing project with equal trepidation.

I soon discovered that Joseph Stumbroski shared the same anxiety. Joe was about five feet four inches tall, with dirty blond hair, an edgy Baltimore accent, and a sophisticated (for his age) sense of style, which seemed odd for a child of working-class parents (a Polish father and an Italian mother). Every day on our trips to and from school, Joe and I would eyeball each other suspiciously, but we never spoke. Until one day, through fate or friction, we bonded or, more accurately, bled together. That day, heading home, I was almost clear of the school parking lot (in those days I thought it was

at least a mile long, but on a recent trip there, I was aston-
ished to realize how small it actually was) when several upperclassmen approached.

"We hate niggers," yelled one of them. The others nodded
in agreement. Just about then, Joe Stumbroski walked past,
and for some reason he stopped. "And we hate nigger lovers
almost as much as we hate niggers."

Joe looked as stunned as I felt. Didn't these jerks realize
that Joe and I were freshmen and that we weren't friends?
Before the upperclassmen could jump us, Joe and I took off.
We ran as hard as we could all the way to the bridge. A small
bridge over a narrow creek, it was the border that separated
the safety of our neighborhood from the segregated communities surrounding it. Joe and I had no idea we lived just a
few blocks from each other. And why should we? He had
gone to an all-white Catholic elementary school and I to a
predominantly black one. We were so overjoyed to reach the
safety of the bridge, we stopped to celebrate.

"I'm Joe. What's your name?" Joe extended his hand, accompanied by a toothy grin.

I returned the gesture. "I'm Byron." But before we could
seal our lifelong bond with a handshake, we were approached
by several "project boys." How could we be so stupid? In
our sprint from danger, we drew the attention of several
teenagers from the housing project. What an odd sight in
East Baltimore in 1974: a black boy and a white boy running
together. "What do we have here? A cracker boy and an
Oreo."

Joe was the cracker, and I was the Oreo (black on the
outside, white on the inside). There was no escaping this

confrontation. Joe and I fought valiantly. Back to back, we fought like warriors against a barrage of racial slurs and fists. When it was over, Joe and I were tossed in the creek with our books. Bloodied and wet, we looked at each other and started to laugh.

"You fight pretty good for a white boy," I said through a bloodied lip.

Joe returned the compliment. "But why didn't you float like a butterfly," he added with a chuckle. From that moment on, we became friends and remain so to this day, and Joe's parents became like my second parents. I can't imagine that Mr. or Mrs. Stumbroski had any black friends, but they treated me and fed me like family. When my mother underwent surgery and was hospitalized for more than a week, Mrs. Stumbroski made dinner for my brother and me every day. She made sure we ate before her own family ate. And every morning during high school, the neighbors on my block could hear her blowing the horn of her car. "I have to make sure my boys get to high school on time," she'd often say. The Stumbroskis always had my back.

Many of my Curley classmates were like brothers, and the priests were more like older brothers and uncles than teachers. The faculty, staff, and administration took an interest in the whole student. It was always an odd and joyous sight every February at all-black New Shiloh Baptist Church to see a half dozen or more white faces in the audience for our annual young adult choir concert. They came all dressed in black, with trench coats covering their robes, just to see me perform. The first year that a handful of priests from Curley came to my church, it caused a minor crisis. As my choir mates and I were lining up in the back of the church to march in that Sunday evening of the concert, someone yelled "What are the police doing here? Black folk can't have anything without white people messing it up."

Several people in the choir and congregation assumed the white guys in the black trench coats were police officers. It was a great lesson about cultural assumptions on both sides. After a few years, my pastor would even acknowledge the priests in the crowd. It was a great source of pride for my entire family that a group of white priests from Archbishop Curley would drive across Baltimore City to attend my concert. For many of the priests, it also became one of the highlights of their yearly social calendar. Some of my friends would joke: "Those priests aren't here for the gospel; all they want is the soul food afterward."

I was lucky to have them there. At an age when many adolescents were challenging authority, I cherished and needed the uncompromising support of these priests. They weren't simply friars or fathers, they had replaced my real father, who by this time had all but slipped out of sight. At least one time that I know of, my mother had asked him to help with a tuition payment, and he never returned the call. While my mother attended every single one of my football and wrestling competitions in high school, I never saw my father's face in the crowd. I always missed his presence and missed the things a father would teach a son. How to tie a tie, polish a pair of shoes, or ask a girl out on a date. I would learn these things from a collection of men.

John Lattimore taught me that a man could be both rugged and well groomed. Mr. Lattimore was the first man I knew who wore a suit and tie to work. He was my mother's co-worker and longtime friend, part of her drinking and gossiping crowd. Her friends would often gather at our house after work, or my mother would meet them at their favorite bar. Mr. Lattimore's brother was a college football coach. He knew how much I adored football, so sports was always an easy topic. He was on the short list of my mother's colleagues who praised her for sending me to Curley and remaining so demanding. I think she always valued his counsel and support. He was well educated and the only person I knew who had a master's degree and had traveled overseas. He set an example for me of the value of a good education. He and my mom were never romantically involved, but I'm certain he chipped in a time or two to make my tuition payments. My senior year in high school he volunteered to let me drive his Cadillac to the prom. A two-door, blue 1977 Cadillac with a temperature-controlled air-conditioning system (that was fancy stuff in 1978) and white-wall tires. I washed it twice, used Armor All on the tires and interior. I almost slipped out of the seat as I drove to pick up my girlfriend. His kindness always stuck with me. It was one of the first rewards I had ever received for simply being a good kid. It made an impression on me. Do right and eventually people will notice.

Coach Cook, Coach Mack, Mr. Lattimore, Joe Stumbroski, Mr. and Mrs. Stumbroski, they all had my back. Despite the economic circumstances and academic deficiencies of my youth, I never felt deprived or shortchanged. God had blessed me with the priceless gift of family and a rainbow of friends. People who in their own ways looked beyond my limitations or the circumstances of the time and gave freely of themselves without any expectation of return on their investment, and they did so time after time. Where would I be without each and every one of them? Some were Baptist, some were Catholic, some professed no religion of any sort, to the best of my knowledge, but there's no doubt they were sent by God. Who's got your back? Do they know how much you value them? Don't wait too long. How I wish I'd shown Coach Mack how much I value him.

FIVE

The Hands That Pull You Up

You can't climb a mountain without some rough spots to hold on to.

—Roberta Mae Walden

ALL THOSE HELPING HANDS could smooth the path, but none could do the work for me. Soon I would discover the difference between those who loved and supported me just the way I was and those who could lead me to who I needed to become. To this point, my coaches and friends and the like had taught me valuable life lessons. They were encouraging and kept my spirits up, never allowing me to dwell in self-pity. But I reached an age when I needed to learn specific skills. In many ways, I was still a very young child trapped in an adolescent's body. What I needed now was structure and academic discipline, because it was still a struggle for me to keep up in school, especially when it came to reading.

Think of all the books you had read by the time you were fourteen or fifteen. Perhaps an adventure series like Tolkien's *Lord of the Rings* or a classic like *To Kill a Mockingbird* or one of Michael Crichton's great science-fiction thrillers. Poetry by Langston Hughes or the sweeping romance of Zora Neale Hurston. Then imagine if you had never read for enjoyment until you were nearly fourteen or fifteen. It would stunt your reading experience and deny you the rich experiences that all those books would have brought you.

That was me. Playing catch-up. Not a natural reader, but with the years I had invested in my reading machine, I was now a careful and deliberate but slow reader. I could quote Scripture, but I was unfamiliar with the flow of the written word. Not only did it take me longer to read, but since I hadn't read as much, I didn't have the same starting point as my classmates. I read a book for the first time cover to cover, simply for pleasure, when I was about fourteen. It was Ernest Hemingway's *Old Man and the Sea*. Can't be certain why I chose it. It might simply have been because I liked Hemingway's beard. Nonetheless, when I told my mother of my plans, she advised me against it.

"Son, why don't you read a simpler book first," she said. Here was the woman who had been my number-one champion showing some doubt.

"What's wrong ?" I asked her.

"I don't want you to get discouraged if the book gets too hard. Why don't you read something else and work your way up to Hemingway."

More than disappointed, I was startled by her reaction. Fortunately for us both, another one of my core qualities kicked in: stubbornness. "I'll read this book because I can read anything," I proclaimed.

Right away I could relate to the old man's struggles

against the marlin and the predatory sharks, as well as the expectations of others. But I would eventually learn there is a dramatic difference between reading and comprehension. I read Hemingway's words at fourteen, but it would actually take years for me to grasp his meaning. Santiago's triumph over adversity, and his struggle with his pride, has certainly resonated with me and my life.

My struggle, along with the shame and embarrassment, has made me angry most of my life. In fact, seething with anger. Jealous, competitive, and sensitive to the slightest insult, I hated anyone who was smarter than I was, which, by the time I got to Archbishop Curley High School, meant almost everybody. Freshman year at Curley I was ranked 310 out of 330 students. More than making me feel inferior to most of my classmates, it made them the enemy. When I wasn't working to improve my grades to please my mother, I was working harder to prove something to the kids around me. Besides Joe Stumbroski, I had very few friends for the first couple of years of high school. Perhaps Joe and I were close because we were never in the same classes. He was never an adversary. I chose to dislike most of my classmates. In an odd way, it made it easier to function. If a classmate got an A and I got a C, it meant that he was better than me, smarter than me, probably laughed at me and therefore could not be trusted. I avoided study groups. I never wanted anyone to know how slowly I read and how slow I was to comprehend. The same whispers and looks of pity or disgust that followed me into the basement at St. Katherine's tagged along in high school. I was in remedial reading. The class for dummies was how it was commonly referred to. Another familiar insult. A class full of adolescent boys, working through their learning disabilities, while, outside, the cool boys preened and teased.

But I managed to keep all my rage inside (or express it on the football field). The best way for me to cope and live within my mother's rules was to "kill them with kindness." It became my motto. A bad student. *A good kid.* A poor reader. *The most polite boy in class.* Slow to comprehend. *He's the hardest worker we've ever seen.* It's been the same approach most of my professional life. Always the underdog, but unfailingly polite and disciplined. One of the coaches at Curley described our football team this way: agile, mobile, and hostile. That was the attitude I took into class. Every slight was noted. I kept score on everything, ready to settle up in due time. Unlike many of the classmates in remedial reading who displayed their anger by becoming discipline problems or mentally punching out of class, mine forced me to emphasize my strengths as I built on my weaknesses.

However, hard work did not guarantee success. I got a D in reading first term and was placed on academic probation. My mother's finesse may have gotten me into Curley, but in order to stay, I'd have to improve my grades. I was ordered to stay after school to work with a reading specialist and meet with my guidance counselor. Once again, disappointment created an opportunity.

Father Bartholomew was a sturdy-looking man, who wore glasses and had thinning blond hair. Though he rarely smiled, he had a pleasant expression on his face. He was my image of what Christ might look like, not his color but his character and gait. He walked with a purpose. He wasn't athletic, but he always looked fit. He wore sandals almost year-round. Father Bart was both practical and encouraging.

He asked a life-changing question: "What's your plan?"

"I want to play pro football," I said with a smile.

He laughed. "That's a nice dream, but what is your plan? What about college? How do you plan on getting there? Your current grades won't get you there. Trade school or community college but not a four-year college." He could see from my expression that this news was saddening to me, so he added, "That's not good news or bad news. That's just where you are."

It was a powerful reality check. It's nice to dream, but you need a way to get there. Father Bart and I first mapped out my four-year plan for high school, and then he said, "Now let's make the plan within the plan. Planning your education, like planning your life, is like building a house one brick at a time. So let's talk about what you have to do today to prepare for college."

That first forty-five-minute session lasted a few hours. Since Father Bart lived only a hallway away in the rectory and I would walk home to an empty house, neither of us was in a hurry. Like an architect at his drafting table, Father Bart laid out everything I'd need to build a "plan within the plan." From his shelf, he pulled out a college directory, which detailed all the entrance requirements. He opened it and pointed at random to the first college he came across and said, "These are the requirements to get in.

"You see," he said, "based on your current schedule, you can't get into this school. We could keep going, but we'd find the same thing almost everywhere." My shoulders rounded with disappointment. "Chin up," he said with confidence, "we've got four years to get you ready."

For the remainder of the session, we pored over my current schedule and coordinated it with the classes I'd need to get into college. It's worth noting he never set boundaries on what kind of college. So at fourteen, still reading below grade level, I was allowed to hold on to the notion of endless possibilities. We went over my syllabus for the remedial reading and math classes, and he described how I would have to progress to get into a so-called good school. Then he went deeper, explaining the kind of time I'd have to put in studying. There were formulas he said for how long good students study.

"You'll have to study even longer and harder," he said. By this point, his tone was more like a football coach. He wasn't quite yelling with excitement, but he was forceful.

We made a schedule for every half hour of my day, from the time I woke up in the morning until bedtime. He arranged for a tutor. He also got me a job mopping the halls after school so that I'd have a reason to be on campus, other than the extra academic help I needed. It remained unspoken, but Father Bart was aware how sensitive I was to being seen as different. The job after school gave me great cover when friends asked, "Why are you hanging around?" Added to that was the fact that my family could use the extra money. I wasn't the only kid whose parent(s) scraped to send their son to Curley. The school had its own work/study program of sorts. After school, boys worked mopping the halls and cleaning classrooms.

The routine suited my mother just fine. Clarice Pitts made

sure I did every extra-credit activity and kept to a strict regimen of school, work, sports practice, homework, and church. My mother didn't allow friends in the house unless she was home. I wasn't allowed to go to anyone else's house other than the Stumbroskis'. House parties were forbidden. I could go to a dance at school or to a church event, but teenage hangouts and the mall were not allowed. I was permitted to go out on Friday nights and was always home by 11:00 P.M. Later in life, my own children and their peers have always found such boundaries barbaric. "Nothing good ever happens after midnight," Clarice often said when I would plead for an extended curfew. Once I gave a well-thought-out rebuttal, "Is that when you and Daddy got married, after midnight?" I thought it was brilliant. She playfully but with an edge punched me in the shoulder. "Don't say that again."

Despite where I was academically, Father Bart never discouraged me. He taught me to know where you are and where you want to go. I wanted to go to college, and Father Bart assured me he would help me get there. In many ways he helped put my reading deficiencies in perspective. I was in remedial reading, but I didn't have to stay there. I could go farther with a plan. It also helped that we always started and finished our meetings with prayer. How wonderful it was for me to be in an environment where prayer was not simply encouraged but expected. All the distance I had traveled to this point came on whispered prayers. Now I was in an environment that affirmed that prayer can take you as far in life as you're willing to plan and work. Who knew Franciscans also believed in the African proverb: When you pray, move your feet.

Gradually I began to improve. There was growing comprehension. I was gaining confidence, though I was still very quiet because of the snickers over my speaking deficiencies. By my sophomore year I had moved out of remedial math and reading. Although I was still closer to the basement than the top of the academic curriculum at Curley, my spirits were buoyed by a sense of accomplishment. Because teachers knew that I was a hard worker, they were willing to spend extra time with me after class. Most were encouraging and supportive. Sports remained the center of my universe, but I was no longer simply surviving in class. I was beginning to thrive. I eventually found a subject I loved—history. From the American Revolution to the Civil War, the stories of conflict and courage appealed to me. I could relate to figures like Crispus Attucks, the first black man reported to have died in the American Revolution. The people around him underestimated his talents, but when the time came, he proved his worth. History had a beginning, middle, and end. That's how I began to see my life. I enjoyed it without prodding from my mother. The more I learned about a given topic, the more I wanted to learn. I was finally reading. And there was a reward. History was the first class in which I ever received an A.

Until this time I was still very much a loner and was afraid to engage in an academic conversation with a classmate or really speak up in a class discussion. But by junior year, especially in history class, there was a gradual recognition by my peers that I excelled in this subject, and they sought my opinion and even my help. This was a new experience for me. I was not accustomed to having a reputation as one of the

This is the earliest photo of me. Looks like I was practicing to hold a microphone even then.

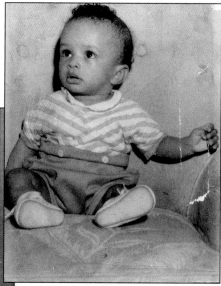

I love this picture of my mother. She looks so glamorous and happy, dressed up to attend a cabaret on board a ship docked at Baltimore's harbor.

My father always dressed well. He was a butcher, but he dressed like a banker.

Photographs courtesy of the author except where noted.

This is me on the front porch of our house on Federal Street. My mother, brother, and I moved out on Christmas morning, 1972.

This is the only photo ever taken of my father and me. I was thirteen years old. He had come by to say hello during the Christmas holiday.

My cousin Kim Walden and me loading up a bucket from my grandmother's well. It was one of my chores during the summers I spent in Apex, North Carolina.

An elementary school photo. Is it any wonder my nickname was Pickle? That's the biggest forehead I have ever seen.

My siblings, Mac and Saundra, and me at age eleven. We were dressed for church.

I took my girlfriend Kim Taylor to the junior prom at Archbishop Curley.

That's Father Bart on the left, with the blond hair. The priests from Archbishop Curley were regular attendees at a gospel concert at my family's Baptist church.

Gene and Gustava Stumbroski, Joe's parents. (*Courtesy of the Stumbroskis*)

A suave James Mack. Everyone called him Coach Mack because he coached swimming and wrestling. (*Courtesy of the Mack family*)

Joe Stumbroski's high school graduation photo. (*Courtesy of Archbishop Curley High School*)

I met Dr. Ülle Lewes on the day I decided to drop out of Ohio Wesleyan (*circa 1980*). (*Courtesy of Dr. Ülle Lewes*)

At Ohio Wesleyan, Peter Holthe gave tours of the Botany Department to local elementary school students. (*Courtesy of Peter Holthe*)

I played defense for the Ohio Wesleyan Bishops for three years. During my senior year, I broke a bone in my hand and sat out the entire season.

The three most important women in my life: my mother, Clarice (*left*), Dr. Ülle Lewes (*center*), and my grandmother, Roberta Mae Walden (*right*), seen on my graduation day, 1982.

My family grows up. Mac lives in Missouri and works as a long-haul truck driver. Saundra got her master's in criminal justice and works for child protective services in North Carolina. Mom was a social worker until her retirement in 1996.

My first reporting job in Greenville, North Carolina. The small paycheck was the best diet plan I've ever known. (*Courtesy of WNCT-TV, Greenville, NC*)

As a great cameraman once said to me: "Don't stand when you can sit and don't sit when you can lie down." I have learned how to sleep anywhere, including on the floor of an airport.

November 2001 in Afghanistan. In the front from left to right: reporter Phil Ittner from CBS Radio, producer Larry Doyle, and cameraman Mark Laganga. Next to me in the back is Bob Martin, a reporter from KRQE in Albuquerque.

From January 2004 until the war with Iraq started in March, I reported from Kuwait. (*Courtesy of CBS News*)

Covering a firefight in downtown Baghdad on the day
Saddam's statue fell. (*Courtesy of CBS News*)

I returned to OWU as commencement speaker in May
2006. Helping me are a very proud Ülle Lewes and Provost
David Robbins. (*Courtesy of Ohio Wesleyan University*)

In Washington, D.C., for President
Obama's inauguration, I'm joined
by producer Daniel Sieberg, sound-
man Craig Anderson, and producer
Rodney Comrie. (*Courtesy of Ben-
son Ginsburg*)

Current time:
06/08/2018,14:
10
Pickup By:
6/19/2018
Title: Step out
on nothing :
how faith and
family helped
Item ID:
3402808591973
7
Pickup library:
KT

"smart" students. Around the same time, my other grades began to improve, and I liked being recognized for something other than athletics.

It was also in my junior year that Curley started a school newspaper and I signed up to be a sports writer. I loved sports, and I was beginning to love words. It seemed like a natural fit. It was the first time someone other than a teacher or relative would read my work. I would sit in the cafeteria and watch classmates read an article I had written. It would make me think back to the days when people thought I was stupid. Now people were reading my stories. Sometimes they would laugh, sometimes they would look surprised, and sometimes they would look pleased or at the very least interested. The fact that I could provide people with critical information gave me the sense that I mattered. I served a purpose.

Along with the academic improvements, I was gradually gaining ground on a normal teenage life. Pickle was growing up. I still stuttered, but I was more comfortable, and confident enough to speak up when I had to and didn't even mind friends who finished my sentences. By senior year, I experienced a respite from my struggles. I was a solid B student, ranked 30 out of a class of 240. Four years earlier I'd been ranked 20 from the bottom. My body had finally caught up with the size of my head. I had a steady girlfriend. Kim Taylor lived at home with her parents and three sisters in a suburban neighborhood. Kim was the perfect high school girlfriend. We had known each other since junior high school, when we sang in the church choir together. We shared similar values, neither of us drank or did drugs, and we could dream aloud about college. In my world outside of Curley, there were not many people who had such dreams.

And getting into college was a priority. For years my mother had warned me, actually threatened me, about what life would be like without an education. I learned exactly what she meant after graduation, when I spent the summer working on a maintenance crew for the Maryland State Department of Transportation. At the time, the law required all summer employees to be at least eighteen years old. It was a good paying job, and our family needed the income, so I lied about my age. I got a job cutting grass along Interstate 95 near the Baltimore Harbor tunnel and cleaning the tollbooths and inside the tunnel tube. It was dirty and somewhat dangerous work. The large self-propelled lawn mowers could cut a three-foot-wide swath of grass, a pile of garbage, or a person's leg. I loved the work. Walking up and down the grassy median of the interstate behind my industrial-strength lawn mower, often under the hot sun, was almost therapeutic. The walking would strengthen my legs for football, and pushing around the lawn mower and lifting debris was as good as lifting weights. It may have been the most instructive job I've ever had.

Every day, twice a day, employees would punch a clock. We could arrive early if we wanted to, but the paycheck would only reflect a change (a deduction) if we were late. I don't remember the names of any of the men I worked with, but I can still see their faces. The foreman was a small, tightly wound white man in his midfifties. His dark pants and orange work shirt were always neatly pressed. Even his black work boots had a nice shine. If not the orange shirt, then the white socks always gave him away. One of the workers in our crew was always responsible for keeping his government-issued white pickup truck clean and the tire rims polished. He had an awful habit of calling all the black crew members Skip. The first time he called me Skip, I walked past him. He pulled my arm and said, "Didn't you hear me, boy?"

"You said Skip, sir. My name is Byron Pitts," I answered.

He looked confused and walked away in a huff. From then on I'd always respond appropriately if he yelled Skip. I took it to mean whichever one of you colored boys is close, come do such and such. There were three other men assigned to our crew full-time (there were several other crews). Two of my crew mates were black and one was white. The white guy had a distinct accent, pure Dundalk (only people from Baltimore have heard it or at least would recognize it), a beer belly, and a perpetual three o'clock shadow. He was always pleasant and, for the most part, minded his own business.

Whenever our day was interrupted by rain and the boss would pick us up, the white guys rode up-front and the brothers back in the flat. There was a constant barrage of harsh language, lots of cigarettes without filter tips, and the frequent liquid lunch if the boss man wasn't around. Since they thought I was older, I had talked about my plans to go to college soon. One payday the white member of our crew yelled at me, "Why are you going to college? You oughta just get a job. I gotta job. And every two weeks my paycheck speaks to me."

Before I could answer, the eldest and quietest member of our crew did something he rarely did when we were in a group; he spoke up. "Leave the boy alone," he said in my defense. He went on to say, "Son, stay in school. Someday your paycheck is gonna scream at you."

We all chuckled. I had a smile on my face the remainder of our shift. I wish I could remember his name. I would work with him for three summers of my life; he was more like a favorite uncle than a co-worker. I never knew if he could read. On those rare occasions when we had to read instructions on a piece of equipment, he'd always ask me to read for him, explaining he'd forgotten his reading glasses. There's no doubt the fourth member of our crew could not read. He had a stutter far worse than mine, and the boss often treated him more like an animal than a man. He never objected. He and I would exchange greetings only in the morning and at the end of the day.

We may have been an odd collection of men, but five days a week, eight and half hours per day, we were together. Thirty minutes for lunch was usually spent under a bridge or on the side of the truck. Ten minutes to eat (I usually carried my familiar bologna sandwich with mustard on white bread) and twenty minutes to nap, either in the shade beneath the bridge or on the ground beneath the truck. Learning to sleep on the side of Interstate 95 (with your back to traffic, of course) would be great training for one of the vital skills of being an international journalist: the ability to sleep anywhere at any time.

There were also tremendous role models for the value of hard, honest work. For some of the men I toiled with that summer, cutting grass on the interstate was the pinnacle of their working lives. It's what they were good at and where they found satisfaction. They maximized the talents God

gave them. That may be hard for many people to understand. My mother was clear about such things. Do your very
best at whatever God has given you to do. Push past what
you think is possible. If that's a perfect shrub in landscaping,
so be it. She saw a different potential in me. Today I work in
a profession with people who are well compensated and well
respected for what they do. Yet many complain about being
overworked, underpaid, and underappreciated. Many of
those men in orange shirts whom I had the honor to work
beside never complained about jobs that paid barely north
of minimum wage. They were decent men who saw dignity
in their work. They didn't make excuses.

I don't look back on those days through rose-colored
glasses. At the end of the workday, my hands and limbs were
sore. I smelled. I was sweaty for hours. Yet there was structure and simplicity to the tasks. Gas the mowers in the morning. Walk north or south behind the mower until it ran out
of gas or it was lunchtime. Fill the tank, and then walk until
the workday was done. In a few days or a few weeks, we'd
reach the end of our section of highway, then we'd simply
turn around and head the other way. It was the Forrest Gump
approach to work. On bad weather days we'd get to clear
trash near the toll plaza, and at least once per summer paint
the booths.

For me, that summer was like a year at prep school. It
crystallized the reasons why I wanted to go to college and
what the alternative would be if I failed. Earlier that spring,
I had been accepted to a few schools—I received average
SAT scores, but I had strong extracurricular activities, which
included football, and glowing recommendations. All those

who wrote letters said pretty much the same thing, "Give this kid a chance."

My mother and I had decided on Ohio Wesleyan University for some of the same reasons she chose Curley, a small school with good academics in a safe, supportive environment. And by safe, I mean middle of nowhere. Delaware, Ohio, is about as far from East Baltimore as one can imagine. One is overwhelmingly black. The other is overwhelmingly white. My mother and I flew to Columbus and took a shuttle van to campus. I wondered to myself, "Am I going to college or a farm?" Nothing looked familiar. East Baltimore is a world of row houses, parked cars, blacktop streets, mixed-breed dogs, and lots of black people. That first day in Ohio I saw more cows than people who looked like me. It took about ten minutes to drive the entire length of the town. The college campus is compact, easy to walk from end to end, with a population of about 2,400 students. About 500 were brand-new, just like me.

My brief taste of college life had been when I was a high school senior on a recruiting trip (not to Ohio). The football players took me to a fraternity party. During the course of the evening, they began to pass a marijuana-filled bong around the room. When my turn came, never having seen a bong before, I did what I thought all the others had done. I blew as hard as I could. Pot sprayed everywhere. All over the floor, the walls, books, even on one of my hosts. To say the least, I made a poor impression. I think the guys would have jumped on me if not for having to explain why a fight broke out on a recruiting trip. Needless to say, I bypassed that school and was never tempted to try pot again, or any other drug, for that matter. I had never heard the term *recreational drug use* until I got to college. In my world back in Baltimore, junkies did drugs and drunks drank alcohol. Their shocked reaction always surprised me when classmates found out I didn't do either.

Since my mother and I arrived before my roommate and his family, I got to stake out the best spot for my belongings. The time alone in the room also helped calm my nerves a bit about meeting him and about living with a stranger for the very first time in my life. I was a football recruit, a full-fledged jock. Usually, those are the most confident characters on campus. I, on the other hand, was a bit of a geek. Not a book-smart geek. But an unworldly young man who thought church choir rehearsal was a great night out.

I had spent weeks thinking about whether or not I would fit in at Ohio Wesleyan University, facing the academic challenges I anticipated and the social pressure I dreaded. I was relieved that Mother had made the trip with me. She helped me unpack. It didn't take long: I had one suitcase and one box. Inside the box was the same stereo my sister had taken to college ten years earlier and my mother's childhood pencil holder. It was just a tin can wrapped in brown paper, but as far as I was concerned, it was a family heirloom. My sister had taken it to college. It was mine now. God willing, someday I'd pass it on to my children. The only other item of value was my Bible. Actually, it was my grandmother's pocket Bible. Most of the pages were dog-eared and worn.

Mom and I said a prayer before she sent me off to football practice that afternoon. Eventually I walked back to my dorm room, where my mother would be waiting, so we could go to dinner and talk about my first day of college. Much to my surprise, Mom was gone. In her place, a letter and a single dollar bill.

Dated August 21, 1978, it read:

Dear Son,

I pray your first team meeting went well. I know how excited and nervous you are to be playing college football. I wish I could have been there. My heart reflects back to your days in Little League in East Point. I was so proud of you then. I am even prouder of you now. Please know I'm sorry I couldn't be here when you returned to your dormitory.

I didn't want you to worry or lose your focus, but I only had enough money for us and your stuff to get to Ohio Wesleyan and then get my butt back to the airport (smile). As you see, I've left you a dollar. I wish I had more to give, but I only have two dollars left in my purse. Like we always have done, we share. So I gave you half of what I had and kept the other half. I know a dollar won't get you much, but God has always met our needs. So know that God will meet your needs today, tonight, and in the years to come.

Byron, you've always been a good boy. Please continue to be that. Be the polite young man I raised you to be. Work hard. Pray hard. Study hard. This is a good school. You will do great things here.

Son, always remember I love you, your sister Saundra loves you, your brother Mac loves you, your grandmother

*loves you, all your aunts and uncles love you. Not a day
will pass when we won't be praying for you and believing
in you.*

Do your best and God will do the rest.

*Love,
Momma*

Mom headed home with a buck . . . and I started college
with my sister's old stereo, my mom's pencil holder, my grandmother's pocket Bible, a dollar, and a tractor-trailer full of
love and prayers. I would need all of it because college was
about to kick my behind in new and unfamiliar ways. In all
honesty, my freshman year in college was the scariest year of
my life. My course load included freshman English, geology
(which I hated), philosophy, introduction to journalism, and
Spanish. Each class required more reading than all of my
classes in high school combined. Nothing unnerved me more
than the daily torture of that pile of books I faced every day.
And there was the realization that my mother was not there
to schedule my day and yell threats or encouragement in my
ear. It was up to me.

But it wasn't just the academic pressure. I was beginning
to feel alone and isolated, in part because of the economic
gap between me and many of my classmates. Even when I
had issues at Curley, we were all blue-collar kids. At OWU I
had a classmate with a BMW. I had never seen one before. A
few messy students whined about missing their housekeepers.
I couldn't tell anyone that my grandmother was a housekeeper.
I had classmates who had traveled the world, spent semes-
ters abroad. At Curley we considered Ocean City, Maryland,

a big excursion. I began to feel resentful, deficient, and overwhelmed. The loner was returning.

But out of the agony of this experience came a friendship forged in battle. For every person who's ever told me, "No, you can't, you're not ready, you're not good enough," God has always brought people like Peter Holthe into my life. Pete lived down the hall from me in our dormitory. Our floor was divided into social groups: the farm boys, the frat boys, and the others. Pete wasn't associated with any group, and as a committed bookworm, he often found himself eating alone in the cafeteria. I was usually alone too. We "others" gradually found our way together. Pete is one of the smartest people I have ever known. He arrived at OWU intent on majoring in the sciences. His parents had hoped he would go to an Ivy league school or one of the nation's top business schools. Pete's dad was a partner in a major accounting firm back in their hometown of Minnetonka, Minnesota. Pete decided to study business and zoology, with advanced degrees in decency and friendship.

"My dad may have thought I was rebelling by going to OWU, and perhaps I was. But I was determined to go my own way. I barely paid attention my senior year in high school but aced my SATs, and that's what got me into OWU."

I remember when Pete told me about his journey to college. I was struck by the notion that his attending Ohio Wesleyan was seen as disappointing by his parents, whereas, for my mom, getting me to OWU was a miracle.

I've always described Pete as the whitest white guy I've ever met. Not just pale white (Nordic white), with reddish hair, but he wore thick glasses and had a formality to him that made him seem more like thirty-eight than eighteen. We hit it off right away. Pete thought I was equally weird.

"Why do you play football?" he asked me one day. "You're not going to play professionally, and you must not be very good at it because every time I see you, you're limping or have a limb in a sling. It doesn't make sense why you'd punish your body for no good reason."

That was Pete—everything needed to make sense to him. He's always been analytical. There's an answer to every problem if only one takes the time and puts in the effort to figure it out. He became a dominant voice in the nightly discussions about politics and world affairs that would take place in our dorm, often in his room. Pete and the other guys would exchange ideas, but I rarely said a word. My verbal contribution would be laughter, a grunt, or an occasional one word assent. Mostly, I just listened. Pete knew I had a problem and had the courage to point it out. Actually, at the time, I thought he was incredibly rude.

"Byron, your vocabulary sucks. Sometimes you talk like you're in grade school. And sometimes you use big words that make no sense. What's your problem?"

By then, I thought I was pretty good at masking my remaining shortcomings. I was an incredibly slow reader, but I studied alone so no one really knew how long it took me to read and comprehend my schoolwork. In a new environment, without the comfort of people who knew me well, I slipped back into my pattern of silence to avoid the shame of stammering and stuttering. I generally limited myself to one- or two-word answers. I was never comfortable speaking outside my very limited range. Hiding my deficiencies was a very comfortable state for me. And now, in a matter of weeks, this wise guy from Minnetonka had penetrated my carefully crafted façade.

When Pete was done verbally undressing me, I wanted to punch him in the mouth.

"Who the hell do you think you're talking to?" I barked.

Pete's reply. "I'm talking to you, my friend. Clearly you have a problem communicating, and I want to help."

I was embarrassed and angry. "What gives you the right to t-t-talk down to me?" I sputtered again.

"I'm not talking down to you. I'm sitting, you're standing, so I can't be talking down to you," Pete said with a smile and the clipped laugh I came to appreciate. "Look," he went on, "I'm your friend, and if I didn't care about you, I wouldn't say anything. I know you're not stupid, though sometimes you sound like it. Be honest, what's wrong? You can trust me."

I had spent so many years hiding behind a curtain of lies and secrecy, it wasn't easy for me to tell the truth. But I did. I confided in Pete, told him how long it had taken me to learn to read, told him about the fear I faced every day in class. How overwhelmed I felt before the mountain of reading that was required. Any freshman year in college is tough, but I felt as if I was starting a race and everyone else had already run the first few laps. Being a slow reader was not my only issue. My inability to communicate in class and speak with my professors in a meaningful way was really slowing me down. I rarely spoke in my classes because I didn't have the confidence to express myself.

Pete was not judgmental; nor did he express any shock or

surprise. His response was simple. "If I can help, I will. If I can't, I'll help you find someone who will." And he did help. "Here's what we'll do," Pete said with confidence. "Every day I will give you a new word from the dictionary. I want you to study it. Then, the next day, say it, spell it, define it, and use it in a sentence—deal?"

"What do you want in return?" I asked.

"Nothing. You'll be my first great college experiment. Let's see how we do." That's pure Pete. He was helping me but wanted it to seem as if I was helping him (though I convinced myself that being friends with a football player probably wasn't the worst thing for Pete's social life). That was our secret. We kept the arrangement to ourselves through a few years of different roommates and a few different girlfriends.

Before long, I was coming up with words, and that always made Pete laugh. Like so many of the wonderful people God brought into my life, Pete taught me more by his actions than he did by his words.

When I struggled in a class, Pete devised a study routine for me. It was his idea for me to take all my notes from class and type them out at night in a separate notebook. "Redundancy is good for you," he said. "Plus, your handwriting sucks."

For the remainder of college, I kept two notebooks for every class. One I took with me to the classroom; the other I kept with its neatly typed pages in my dorm room over my desk, and that's the one I would use for studying. As hard as I worked, though, I couldn't match his ferocious and disciplined study habits. Pete studied every night except Fridays. That was his drinking night. Pete knew his way around a chemistry lab and a beer bottle. It was the one area I could keep him in check.

"Pete, what's our limit on beer tonight?" As a nondrinker, by "our" I actually meant "his." Always loyal and always honest, whatever number of beers we'd agree to, that's how many Pete would drink. By Saturday he was back to his books, and on Sundays he read the Sunday *New York Times* from cover to cover. (The only time I ever saw Pete angry was when someone touched the *Times* before he got through reading it.) I just marveled at this guy, my age, taking such enjoyment out of reading everything from textbooks to magazines and newspapers. Not to mention the effort. Since *The New York Times* wasn't delivered on campus, Pete had to walk at least a mile to the store and buy it. Though he was never a fan of exercise, Pete's devotion to making that walk in rain, sleet, or snow on Sundays was impressive. I was never able to convince him to go with me to church on Sunday, and he never got me to read the Sunday *New York Times* either.

Our freshman year in college he was already talking about graduate school and his career, and not in broad terms. He already knew the best schools in the country for his particular discipline, the grades required to get in, and the names of the department heads. Grad school was still three or more years away, but Pete already had a plan. Perhaps Pete was actually Catholic and had a Father Bart back in Minnesota, I often thought to myself. I was already considering my career, too—journalism, believe it or not. Having written for my high school newspaper, I somehow had fooled myself into thinking I might be a pretty good writer. Despite my limited vocabulary, I enjoyed words and expressing myself. So much had been bottled up inside me for the years I couldn't read that I welcomed any chance to read and write. My English teacher in freshman year was Dr. Paul Lucas, who had been at OWU for decades. He was both a brilliant English professor and an unforgiving taskmaster. A tall, thin, balding, pipe smoker, who seemed fond of sweater vests in and out of season, he carried himself like a man who got lost on his way to teach class at Harvard. I had heard Dr. Lucas was tough. I was on a first-name basis with tough, but I still wasn't ready for him. Perhaps he had his favorites, but I seemed to play the role of his whipping post.

He kept his classroom as he carried himself, neat and orderly. He had us working out of small blue notebooks. He didn't want black or gray or brown. He wanted blue. He was meticulous about grammar and proper punctuation. My classmates and I were told early on how he wanted assignments written; the details included which side of the page for our names and the date. No exceptions. I was used to order. Many of my teachers back at Curley insisted a student stand up before giving an answer. We walked on the right side of the hallway and the staircase. I understood order. College was far different from high school. More reading. More freedom. More was expected. I got all that. Dr. Lucas I never got.

"Fine work, Mr. Pitts," he'd say as he handed me an assignment in class marked with a D, if I was lucky, or an F, quite often. Visits to his office were humiliating and often painful. Dr. Lucas pulling on his pipe, puffing smoke as he critiqued my work: lousy grammar, terrible spelling, poor sentence structure, and poor composition. I was befuddled by little things. Because I didn't know how to type and couldn't afford to pay anyone to type my papers, it would take a painstaking amount of time to finish my work. That sometimes meant the essays were not well thought out or corrected. Sometimes papers were simply turned in late. There was no extra credit, and unlike high school, there was no acknowledgment for effort. The sessions went quickly. Dr. Lucas never offered suggestions on how to improve, only criticism. It was clear that he expected my baseline of understanding to be higher than it was. Because I wasn't very verbal, I wasn't equipped to say what I needed. My only response was that "I'm doing the best I can." It got so bad Clarice tried to intervene, eight hundred miles away, from back in Baltimore. Tired of my tearful phone calls home, she called Dr. Lucas directly. I don't think he was accustomed to getting phone calls from parents. Certainly not someone like Clarice Pitts. Her counsel to me, just keep praying and working hard, didn't seem to work. Despite my mother's encouraging words and prayers and Pete's study tips, I failed Dr. Lucas's class and did poorly in several others.

At the end of my first semester in college, I was on academic probation. Another poor showing next semester and I might be kicked out of school. Perhaps as testament to my stubbornness or stupidity, I signed up for Dr. Lucas again. I thought if I was more disciplined with my time and worked harder, I could pass the class. There was no guarantee that another professor was going to be any easier. I believed that the problem was my effort, not his teaching.

After a wonderful Christmas break of home-cooked meals, visits to my church, and time with Kim Taylor, I came back to OWU refueled and ready to conquer the world. I had been down before, but Dr. Lucas seemed to be waiting to take me down another notch every day. So I prayed harder, typed longer, and studied more notes.

When a crucial midterm exam was approaching, Pete worked with me, and my mother made more than her routine phone calls. More nerve-wracking than the actual exam was the day when Dr. Lucas would pass out the results. Nervously waiting near the back of class, my palms sweating, my academic future on the line, I watched and listened as Dr. Lucas passed out papers and puffed on his pipe. Finally, he came to me. Instead of continuing on with the rhythm of passing out papers and moving along, Dr. Lucas stopped at my desk. With a big smile, he placed my test results on my desk and announced to the class, "Congratulations, Mr. Pitts, your best work thus far. D plus. Bravo!"

He proceeded to pass out the remaining few papers to my other classmates. As for me, I was back in my father's car: silent, warm, staring straight ahead, expressionless. I put my hands under my chin and refused to cry or get angry. I never heard another sound the rest of the class. I didn't even realize class was over until my classmates started to leave.

On my way out, Dr. Lucas asked me to follow him to his office. Raised to always respect authority, I gave the only response I knew to give, "Yes, sir." Once I was in his office, Dr. Lucas said what he had to say quickly. At the time it seemed almost kind.

"Mr. Pitts, I'll make this quick. No need to sit down." Rarely did Dr. Lucas ever look directly at me when he spoke, but this time he made an exception. "Mr. Pitts, you are wasting my time and the government's money. You are not Ohio Wesleyan University material. I think you should leave." I had no reaction. He continued. "You're excused. Nothing further. Please tell your mother what I said. Good luck to both of you. Now excuse me."

That's it. Game over. I was done. Hard work and prayer had taken me as far as it could. This professor in a position to know had declared my fate.

What did he mean by "the government's money"? I had received a few grants and scholarships, but he made it sound as if I was on some college welfare program. More than anything else, I wanted to simply be able to walk out of his office with my head still up. I wouldn't give him the satisfaction of seeing me cry. But, at that moment, in the mind of an eighteen-year-old kid, my pursuit of a college education was over. My dreams, my family's dreams, were just that. Perhaps I wasn't retarded or mentally ill, but I was far from college material.

All of our work—the village that pulled me through— those who cheered for me and mentored me and tutored me, for whom I was the hope of a college success story. I had failed them all. This man said I wasn't good enough, and I had to believe that he was right.

At this moment, I was alone and frightened. To this point in life, through every hardship and obstacle, I had had someone who cared about me close by to pick me up, dust me off, and lead me on my way. Always in the past, my mother was in the next room, or there would be an inspiring sermon from Reverend Carter at New Shiloh or an encouraging word from Coach Mack or Father Bart that would lighten my burden and I could push through. This time none of them was in sight. The shame inside me grew. All those demons of insecurity and uncertainty waiting just below the surface of my life were pushing their way to the top. I was ashamed that I had failed, ashamed even more that I was thinking about giving up, quitting.

SIX

Letters from Home

To get where you want to go, you must keep on keeping on.
—Norman Vincent Peale

FOR EIGHTEEN YEARS CLARICE Pitts seamlessly raised me by combining a fierce demand for discipline and an equal measure of love. With the balance of a high-wire acrobat, she would dish out punishment with the same hand she used to hold her children when they needed comfort. Clarice was born with long limbs, but they could not stretch easily from East Baltimore to Delaware, Ohio. The miles between us now created distance and difficulties. My grades were suffering, and I was on the verge of flunking out. In her own way, she still needed to wage the fight for me, just the way she did when I was a kid. She had appealed to Dr. Lucas by phone and was left frustrated. She was not in the habit of being ignored. So perhaps in order to stay connected and still yield a high level of influence, she resorted to writing letters. She is not a casual woman; thus, these would not be casual letters.

School was tough. Clarice was tougher. It was her way of being supportive. To her, support meant brutal honesty. But now the opponent was my own lethargy and intellectual paralysis. If she had to punch through my soul to knock out the enemy, she'd do it.

While it may be hard for my children or many of their generation to believe, long before e-mails, text messages, or cell phones, people communicated regularly by hand-written letters. During my four years in college in the late 1970s, my family and I rarely talked by phone. It was too expensive. There was a pay phone at the end of the hallway in my freshman dormitory, but phone calls were sporadic. A roll of quarters would give me a few minutes on the phone with my mom, a call to my grandmother, and maybe a few minutes on the phone with my sister or girlfriend, Kim. But I could always count on at least one letter per week from my home. Between my freshman year and graduation, my mother must have written me at least 152 letters, one for every week I was in school. Included with each letter, in every envelope, would be a Bible verse typed on an index card. Occasionally, a second index card would hold some encouraging quotation she'd picked up somewhere. Things like: "It is not your aptitude, but your attitude that determines your altitude." She got a lot of these pithy self-help bromides from her new collection of books. Her dozens and dozens of letters became a minor sensation among many of my friends. Especially Pete. He jokingly began referring to my mother as Mother Clarice (as in Mother Teresa) and Colonel Clarice. He found it amusing that this black woman hundreds of miles away seemed to have so much influence over my life. A small circle of friends who were estranged from their own parents seemed to take real joy in her words. Her typed index cards often wound up tacked to the corkboard wall in someone else's room. I've kept many of them. I wish I'd kept them all.

Of all her letters to me and my siblings, the one that's taken on near-legendary status in our family was the one that came in the midst of my struggles with my freshman English professor, Dr. Lucas. My confidence had slipped as much as my grades, and in a few of my phone calls I started dropping hints that maybe OWU wasn't right for me. My mother was not a quitter. She wasn't having it.

Clarice had a unique system for identifying the purpose of her letters even before you read them. Black ink meant all was fine with the world, and there might even be some humor in her correspondence. Blue ink meant she wanted to discuss some difficulty in her own life, which she was more likely to share as her children got older. But if a letter from home came in red ink, that meant the recipient was in serious trouble. Red meant anger. So when the envelope arrived in my dormitory mailbox with my name and address written in red, I knew I was in for a verbal assault, a linguistic beat down. Her first line cleared up any doubt. Clarice Pitts has loved the Lord nearly all of her life, but she's always had great affection for profanity when it served her, especially when it came to making a point to her children.

Dear Mr. Brain Dead,

Have you lost your fucking mind? You went to Ohio Wesleyan with the expressed goal of graduating, going on to live your dreams and God's purpose for your life. At the first sign of trouble you want to give up. Fine! Bring your ass back to Baltimore and get a job. Maybe if you think you're up for it, enroll in Bay College. There are plenty of places in the city for dummies. Yep, come home with your tail between your legs and get some half-ass job and spend the rest of your life crying about what you could have been. Maybe all you're cut out to be is a meat-cutting, cab-driving underachiever. Maybe I was wrong about you. Maybe you have worked as hard as you can, as you claim, and your best isn't good enough. Is that what you think? Here's what I know.

You are a gift from God. The Lord I serve does not make mistakes. You did not get to Ohio Wesleyan because you are so smart or worked so hard. You got there because of prayer and faith and God's grace. Yes, you worked hard in high school. But you only did part of the work. Every time you took one step, God took two. Is college harder than high school? It better be, as much as it cost. So what's that mean for you? Work harder than you think you are even capable of working. Pray longer than you've ever prayed. That's what I'm doing. That is what we always do. What has your grandmother told you? You can't climb that mountain without some rough spots. Maybe you're in a cave on the other side of your mountain. Don't get scared or lazy. Don't just cry. Figure out what God is teaching you, then get your ass back on that mountain and keep pulling hard and looking forward.

Son, you know your momma loves you. I believe in

you. I pray for you. I know you better than you know yourself. And I know a God who is able. You're not coming home. You're not going to give up. You're not going to fail. You are going to endure.

Love,
Mom

Whew! That's my momma summed up in a single letter: angry, passionate, relentless, unbending, unedited, unforgiving, immovable in her faith, and unwilling to give an inch or give up on her son. Regardless of the times, whether or not the experts, the people around her, or even I doubted what was possible, she stood like stone. Thirty years later, it still makes me laugh a bit, even tear up every time I read this particular letter. She never simply pushed—she lifted. I know that now; I sensed it then. As I recall, back in 1978, I had three reactions. As I was reading the letter, I was crying, for obvious reasons, because it felt like she was piling on. It was symbolic of the tension between a kid growing into manhood and his mother. She didn't understand that I was trying.

Then it made me angry. Oftentimes my mother's tough love brought us together. This time it pushed us apart. I understood her point, but she was wrong about the particulars. Up until that point in my life, she had been right about everything.

I remember reading the letter again and finally it made me laugh. It reminded me how intense my mother is. As I read the letter over again and again, it was like looking in a mirror. I too was tough. It was okay to get angry, perhaps even curse a bit, then settle down, refocus, recommit, remember not simply who I was but whose I was. As always, included in the envelope was an index card with Scripture. Psalm 37: "Fret not thyself because of evildoers . . . For they shall soon be cut down like the grass, and wither as the green herb." I wasn't sure if that biblical threat was aimed at me or Dr. Lucas. Mom would later explain that negative thoughts and pessimism were like "evildoers." She was saying don't worry about things. Her bottom line was always, let God fight your battles.

Maybe it was the training that came with being a social worker or the innate skills of a good parent, but even when she was at her harshest, Clarice always seemed to know what was needed and when it was needed. She made a compelling argument. Did I want to return to Baltimore and cut grass on the interstate? Was I giving up? For weeks Clarice continued to write letters of encouragement while I wrestled with the decision to withdraw from school.

My mother was appealing to the dream of who she thought I could be. But Dr. Lucas spoke directly to who I believed I was. "You're not Ohio Wesleyan material," he had said.

My mother was being hopeful. But, in my mind, he was being realistic, more honest. Finally, I was exhausted and wanted to escape them both. If I left school, I would be done with him, and if I went back to Baltimore, I couldn't stay in my mother's house. On a chilly February morning I walked over to University Hall to pick up the forms to withdraw from Ohio Wesleyan.

Sitting on a bench outside, I had my book bag on one

shoulder and blank forms in my free hand. Somewhere between sadness and anger, my emotions provided insulation from the winter cold. I didn't seem to notice the temperature or that I was now crying. Not small tears, mind you, but nose-running, lose my breath, shoulders-shaking tears. How pathetic I must have looked. I guess that's why a plump woman with long brown hair and a heavy coat stopped in front of me.

"Young man, are you okay?" came a slightly accented voice.

"Yes, ma'am, I'm fi . . . fi . . . fine." It was almost guaranteed that whenever I was overcome by emotion, the stuttering would start.

"You don't look fine. Please tell me what's wrong," she insisted. By this time my spirit was broken, and I was too emotionally spent to make up a story, so I just started blabbing. I must have talked for several minutes because the woman in the big coat interrupted me and said, "May I sit down while you continue your story?"

I continued to ramble on for at least twenty minutes. This round-faced stranger just kept smiling and listening. Her body language assured me that what I had to say was somehow important. First I told her what Dr. Lucas had said, that I wasn't college material. I was failing his class, and it was his recommendation that I leave. "I guess I'm just stupid," I told her. "I was fooling myself to think I could make it here." I told her that I was tired of being embarrassed in class. But I knew that if I dropped out of school, it would embarrass my family. I told her I didn't feel as if I had any choice. All the while I was crying, sniffling, and stuttering.

Eventually she interrupted me and said, "I'm so sorry, but I must get back to work now. But can we continue our talk tomorrow. And promise me you won't drop out of school before we talk?"

"Bu ... bu ... bu ... but I'm just stupid. I don't belong here," I mumbled.

Then she flashed a part of her personality I would come to see plenty of in the years to come: "That's just nonsense. Stop it. Stop that right now! Now give me your word you will speak to me tomorrow before you make any final decision on school! Give me your word! Look me in the eye and give me your word!"

Confused about why this stranger would be raising her voice at me, I simply said, "Yes, ma'am."

"Well, good," she answered with a reassuring smile. "My name is Ülle. My office is on the second floor of Slocum Hall. Can you come see me at around eleven?"

"Yes, ma'am."

"Then it is settled. Go on with the rest of your day, and we will speak tomorrow."

I welcomed the chance to delay what seemed like the inevitable. Clarice was always big on going to bed and allowing trouble to rest the night as well. Somehow I felt a bit relieved and finished the day. The next morning I made my way to Slocum Hall. Perhaps because of my own emotional state or her odd accent, I wasn't sure I caught her name correctly. Ohio Wesleyan is a small and friendly campus, and most people could put a name with a face. She did say second floor. Inside Slocum, I asked a student, "Do you know a lady who works in this building—she has long brown hair, friendly round face, a bit on the plump side . . ." (There are a number of plump women in my family, and "plump" was always the preferred description).

"Oh, you mean Dr. Lewes," the student responded.

I smiled. She must be mistaken. "No, this lady isn't a doctor." I thought to myself that maybe she was on the University staff in some capacity. Perhaps administrative or something clerical. Professors, I believed, looked and acted like Dr. Lucas.

"Well, you just described Dr. Lewes. Around the corner on the right. I gotta go."

With that, I was alone in the hallway with directions to a professor's office who couldn't possibly be the woman who listened to my sad and lengthy story the day before. Since I had nothing to lose, I walked to the office as directed, and there to my surprise on the door was the name DR. ÜLLE LEWES. Inside the office, behind the desk, was the plump woman with long wavy brown hair, her face buried in a book. With a knock at the door, I asked, "Dr. Lewes?"

"Good morning, young man," she answered with that familiar smile. "Please come in." It was a greeting that would change my life. The remarkable Dr. Ülle Lewes. If ever I doubted that angels really do exist, those doubts were now cast aside. In time, she didn't simply change my life—she saved it.

SEVEN

An Angel from Estonia

. . . he shall send his angel . . .

—Genesis 24:7

ÜLLE LEWES RECOGNIZED MY struggle because she has
survived a lifetime of her own struggles. I've never been to
Estonia, but in my eyes Ülle Erika Lewes is the embodiment
of her native land. Proud but not boastful, optimistic yet a
realist, tough but easily wounded, loyal but at times distant,
independent but willfully vulnerable, always prepared to fight
for what she loves, and willing to love based on blind faith.
She is like all the women I love. An inner beauty cast inside
an outer toughness. A beating heart wrapped in warm steel.
Open to all but truly welcoming only to a few.

Ülle was born in Tallinn, Estonia, during World War II,
when the country was caught in the middle, with the Soviet
Union pulling and bombing from one direction and Germany
pulling and bombing from the other. Her earliest memories
of childhood were running into the basement with her mother

during aerial attacks by both sides. At the age of three, with her father off fighting the war, Ülle and her mother, grandmother, aunt, and a cousin escaped from Estonia on a barge. They eventually became refugees, first in Latvia, then Lithuania, Poland, Czechoslovakia, and finally in Germany. It was there that she took her first bitter taste of discrimination. She went to school with German kids who hated the foreigners. Surrounded by prejudice, Ülle would pass by police checkpoints and soldiers every day going to and from school. The innocence of childhood and each new day were often interrupted by slurs and intimidation. Her tales of life in a distant world drew me closer to her. The difficulties she had to overcome put my own in a new perspective.

Eventually, in November 1951, Ülle and her family would immigrate to the United States, with the promise of a better life. Sponsored by the Lutheran church for the first six months, they settled in Roxbury, Massachusetts. But amid the promise of the New World was an old and familiar problem: prejudice. On the postwar streets of a Germany scarred in battle, people had hated the Estonian girl because she was foreign. In the racially segregated city of Boston, on the awkward side of the civil rights era, black kids hated the nine-year-old white girl, who did not look like them or sound like them.

When she first came to the United States, it was the same as it was in Germany, the mean looks and crazy questions. But Ülle found peace and comfort in her schoolbooks and in words. Eventually, her family moved to Buffalo, where she graduated valedictorian of her high school class and earned a full scholarship to Cornell. She was fluent in Estonian, Spanish, French, Latin, and German. Ülle's first love was comparative literature. Soon the little girl from Estonia found her path. After graduate school at Harvard University and a brief time teaching at Temple University in Philadelphia, Dr. Ülle Lewes took a job in the English Department at Ohio Wesleyan University.

When I met her, Ülle was a full-figured woman, with thick, curly, reddish brown hair, round glasses, and a perpetual smile. Even on those days when her knees hurt or life did not treat her kindly, there was that smile tickling her eyes and stretching across her kind face, along her soft round shoulders down to the tips of her fingers. She was born to teach English. She taught it the way a good masseuse gives massages: with her entire body. During lectures she would actually extend her arms in the air, rub her fingers together like a sculptor rolling clay, as if the words were alive in her hands. That was Ülle, working to become one with the right word.

She started at OWU in the fall of 1978, the same as me. "I was a new-bee," she said, describing those early days. And soon the "new-bee" from Estonia and the freshman from Baltimore would cross paths on a cold morning outside University Hall. Perhaps it was Ülle's own encounters with disappointment or her feelings of being out of place that allowed her to notice me. Although Ülle has never considered herself a religious person, she acknowledges that some sort of spiritual guidance might have been at work.

At that first meeting in her office she made a commitment to help me. We planned to meet for two hours a week at first, and eventually it increased to three and then four hours. We would get together either in her office or in the Writing Resource Center set up across campus. In the early days, as I struggled with an English assignment, complaining and voicing doubt, she always reassured me. Ülle identified my two basic problems: not enough attention to (as she called them) stupid details; the other, a simple lack of structure. She began to work on my structure issues by organizing my life. Ülle never taught me a single class my freshman year, but she was the only professor I cared about pleasing. She set up something that resembled a shadow class to my scheduled English class. In one hour Professor Lucas would strip at my confidence like a craftsman stripping varnish off an old floor. I would go to Professor Lewes for a new coat of confidence. She rarely questioned the content of my work. She would patiently have me correct punctuation, grammar, and sentence structure. She insisted I pay attention to every detail. Secretly she would grade Dr. Lucas's papers with her own grading scale. While Dr. Lucas was still giving me Ds and Fs, Ülle would grade the same assignment and give it As or Bs. Dr. Lucas measured the outcome, and there was simply a right or wrong, black or white. Ülle graded in the gray area. She measured effort, creativity, and the slightest improvement from the previous assignment.

"He graded you on surface areas like punctuation and sentence structure. It's all important, of course. I graded you on rhetorical structure, development, and detail. Detail provides those vivid nuggets," she said.

With the improvements I was making, by the end of the semester, Dr. Lucas would mark my papers with Bs and Cs and an occasional A. Dr. Lewes, on the other hand, had changed her standards, and suddenly she was giving Cs and Ds. She had helped break Dr. Lucas's code, his standard. Now she was teaching me to set my own and continually move the bar higher.

"Never settle. Push! Push! Push harder."

Ülle showed the sort of kindness, optimism, and concern I had seen in only a handful of people till this stage of my life. She and my mother were from completely different worlds, but they shared this relentless faith in me and in hard work. Both would flash their tempers, not at results but at lackluster effort. Both would use profanity to lecture but never once to scold. It is a characteristic they shared with my favorite athletic coaches. And Ülle seemed inexhaustible. We would often meet at the end of a day after she had taught several classes and met with several other students.

When you are in Ülle's presence, you have her undivided attention. It was during one of those sessions that Ülle touched my hand and shouted, "Look at me! Someday you will write a book." I was eighteen, on academic probation, and a breath away from flunking out of college. A book seemed beyond impossible.

The closer we became as professor and student, the more she sounded like Clarice. I do recall at least one F from Dr. Lewes. On at least one occasion, she did not like my effort.

"Don't get lazy," she snapped. It was as if she had cut me with a knife. Laziness was rarely my problem, but impatience often got the best of me in college and in the years that followed. Why am I still struggling? Why do I still comprehend things so slowly? Why can't I read a chapter once and grasp its meaning? There were times I wanted to give up, not because I was lazy but rather because I was overwhelmed by impatience. The two-step forward one-step back dance often became tiresome. Ülle would always push me past those moments.

"Anyone who reads your work carefully can see you have a brilliant mind," Ülle said. "You have to make them see it and I will help you." Instructive and encouraging. That was her style. Over many years and a few meals, we have discussed Dr. Lucas. What could she see that he could not? "I don't know," she would answer modestly.

To his credit, Dr. Lucas had a wonderful reputation for working with and inspiring honor students. In fact, he was one of the leading advocates for raising the academic standards at Ohio Wesleyan. Standards quite frankly that would have kept me from ever being admitted to OWU. I am sure there are countless OWU grads who can attest to his brilliance and care. That is not my testimony or that of at least two other OWU graduates I've met over the years. Twice while giving speeches around the country, where I told the story of my experience at Ohio Wesleyan and without mentioning his name, a person in the audience would walk up to me afterward, shake my hand, and ask, "Were you talking about Dr. Lucas?" I guess I wasn't alone. We would exchange notes and quickly come to the conclusion that the experience only made us stronger. Perhaps it just serves to illustrate that even in a place as small as Ohio Wesleyan, there are the right people and the wrong people placed in a person's path. You must survive one and cling to the other. I was in Dr. Lucas's class, but I was never one of his students. That first year I was not in a single one of Ülle's classes, but I was most certainly one of her students.

As often as she would allow it, I would eat my lunch in Dr. Lewes's office. Sometimes she was there. Sometimes she wasn't. Her office had become my second home. There were even times I would sit outside her classroom and do my homework. Even her encouraging words aimed at other students would lift my spirits.

Ülle and my mother first met by phone and hit it off instantly, although there was some adjustment required in the beginning because college professors are not used to being treated like daycare providers. Clarice has always taken great pride in keeping tabs on her children. She has called teachers, professors, and a few news directors whenever she has seen fit. One of the few who never seemed to mind was Ülle. "Once your mother called me and asked, 'How is my boy doing? Is he getting an A?' I said no, but if he works hard he may get an A-," recalled Ülle. "She really wanted to understand. I liked Clarice right from the start. She wasn't pushing me—she wanted to understand. Her tone was, I want to understand what's going on. I could sense her heart," Ülle said of my mother.

Two women from different worlds who endured different hardships and whose paths intersected. There have been countless strong women in my life: my mother, sister, grandmother, aunts, and my wife. I revere Ülle Lewes as much as I do any of them. Others have been bonded to me by blood or marriage, but Ülle just showed up one day and never left. Because of her, I believe in angels.

While some students found Dr. Lewes's style odd, pushy,

and invasive, she did teach one course that was a particular favorite. Advanced English Composition. It was a class in which profanity was encouraged. Early in the semester Dr. Lewes would have us close our textbooks, and she would ask us to scream. Then scream and curse. Initially, students were reluctant and shy. Eventually, they would embrace the concept. Before long, she would have to temper their enthusiasm.

"I want to break you down," is how Dr. Lewes described it. "It takes half the semester to break students down. They're so stiff and proper, they're not writing authentically. Just writing school shit and not writing real shit. There is absolutely nothing worse than school talk. Almost all the talk we talk is fake talk. There is nothing wrong with curse words. They're only words. I want my students to write authentically. You can decide if it's [profanity] not proper for the audience and change, but first it must be raw."

I remember the experience. It was both frightening and fun. I had never, not once, cursed intentionally in front of an adult. Dr. Lewes always seemed to value effort and authenticity; perhaps that's why she questioned my occasional speech pattern. Thus far, I stuttered only when I was nervous, angry, or tired. I was never any of that around Dr. Lewes, but occasionally my enthusiasm would get the best of me, and I'd stutter, if only just a bit.

"I thought you were faking some odd British accent or something," Ülle would say many years later.

I believe God equips us all with different gifts and just a select number of them. Ülle Lewes's command of the written word would help shape and change my life. For stuttering, I had to go elsewhere. Fortunately for me, help with stuttering was actually in the next building. If Dr. Lewes was all things kind and encouraging, Dr. Ed Robinson was all things cranky and gruff. He was a professor in the understaffed, less-than-glamorous department of speech communications at Ohio Wesleyan. Simply put, it was a department few people on campus seemed to take seriously at the time. Dr. Robinson was a bear of a man. A few inches over six feet tall and with a thick Midwestern build, he was more old lion than cuddly teddy bear. His voice was just as loud and scratchy as the Harley-Davidson motorcycle he rode to campus. At a university where some professors rode bicycles, walked, or drove fuel-efficient cars, the sight of Dr. Robinson riding his Harley was often greeted with a turned-up nose or rolling of the eyes. Oddly enough, he always seemed to have a soft spot for the inner-city kid who, like him, didn't seem to fit in at this small liberal arts college in Ohio.

"I like you, Pitts," he'd say. "You're a tough kid."

Dr. Robinson noticed my problem with stuttering one day when he asked each student to declare what they wanted to do for a career after college. Many of my classmates were children of privilege or came from stable middle-class families. Their career plans seemed consistent with their upbringing. Some answered with ease and conviction. "I will be a teacher.... A lawyer.... I will work in my dad's company...." When it was my turn, I said, "I want to be a jour ... jour ... jour ... journalist." I could hear the whispered laughter around me. With a stone cold stare, Dr. Robinson looked at me and said, "See me after class."

Expecting harsh advice from yet another unyielding professor, I braced myself for Dr. Robinson's comments. "How long have you stuttered?" he asked.

"Sir?" I answered.

"You heard me—how long have you stuttered?" Dr. Robinson wasn't into pleasantries or repeating himself. "I think I can help you." That's all he ever said. It was a quick glimpse of kindness he would never betray again. I wish now that I had been looking directly in his eyes because perhaps they would have revealed more. Except for those six words "I think I can help you," I had all but missed a precious moment with a man who had joined the list of those who would change my life.

For the next year or so, Dr. Robinson, with the help of a colleague of his from Ohio State, worked with me patiently. He would force me to sit in a booth at the radio station for thirty minutes at a time and record my voice. The recording was easy. Speaking with pencils in my mouth was the challenge. There was no money in his budget to teach speech pathology, and I did not have the money or the means to drive to Ohio State University in Columbus, which had the resources I needed. So, with Dr. Robinson's help, we improvised. He would have me read Shakespeare or the sports page forward and backward. He insisted I take a theater course called The Actor's Voice. He also encouraged me to take on a hosting job at the radio station. Odd choice for a stutterer, but he believed in confronting the problem. And it worked. I never stuttered on the air. I used a technique of singing my sentences. It helped me transition between the words without taking a breath. I likened it to church, where the minister sometimes sings the words in a sermon. I did the same thing with my scripts. (It was a habit I had to break years later as a professional journalist.)

"You gotta keep working, keep practicing," he insisted. "You can lick this if you work at it," he'd say more as an order than as words of encouragement. I would often greet his directives with a smile. If I closed my eyes, ignored the smell of his cologne and the scratchy bass in his voice, he too sounded like my mother. Often my smile would turn into a brief and quiet laugh.

"Concentrate! Slow down! Breathe!" That was as detailed as his coaching ever was. I suspect he had little or no training as a speech pathologist. In the same way, he was not a trained motorcycle mechanic, but he tinkered and cursed over his Harley-Davidson and kept it on the road. Much the same way, he kept me on the path God was paving for me. Through the years I have talked with skilled speech pathologists who talk about the dark ages of working with people who stutter. Many of the things Dr. Robinson had me do were long ago cast aside as outdated. Today, there are a number of institutions across the country that work faithfully and skillfully with people of all ages who stutter. There are even associations for people who stutter. I have done a few news stories on stuttering but have never sought specialized training. I could certainly still use it. There are words with which I still struggle. Phrases I avoid. It has forced me, as best I can, to think before I speak. It has left me vulnerable in verbal confrontations. But the practice of pausing and gathering my thoughts before speaking has served me well as a journalist.

Life is always about choices. The choices we make for ourselves and the choices people make for us. Dr. Robinson and I lost contact. He left Ohio Wesleyan not long after I graduated. Some people saw him as bitter and outdated. His old school ways and unpolished manner suited me perfectly. I believe we are all instruments of God. There aren't many uses in life for an old rusty hacksaw, except when only an old rusty hacksaw will do.

Dr. Lewes and I continued our tutoring sessions for well over a year, but by the end of my sophomore year, most of my visits to Dr. Lewes's office were more social than academic. I'd go by her office for lunch, and we would shoot the breeze, sometimes talking about her life and not my academics at all. By now she was becoming my friend. She had helped me unlock Dr. Lucas's system, and she'd taught me to do two things that applied to every class: meet the instructor's expectations and do my best. Before college, my teachers and tutors and counselors had always come to my level to figure out my problems. What Ülle taught me was that now I had to meet the professors at their level. I had to learn to interpret what each professor needed and to deliver it, not always plead with them to help me understand or give it to me in smaller bits so I could digest it.

I began to select classes based not just on the credits I needed but on professors to whose style I could adapt. I even avoided the professors who had a reputation for easier courses because I recognized the need to challenge myself in as broad a way as possible. I had a philosophy professor my sophomore and junior years who loved his students to be engaged in class, challenging him in the discussion. So I would prepare for his class by having mock discussions in my dorm room, sometimes alone, sometimes with Pete. Spelling was a challenge, too. In the journalism department, one professor would give a red F for misspelling someone's name, lowering your grade by a full letter. Two red Fs and you could easily fail the class. Before Ülle, that kind of standard would have intimidated me, but after Ülle's counsel, I embraced it. Once I understood his standard, I worked harder to achieve it. Steadily my grades in all my classes began to improve.

With an unbreakable bond and affection, Dr. Ülle Lewes quickly became a permanent part of my family. She wept with my mother at my graduation and years later attended my wedding as a member of my family. The weekend my wife and I got married we threw two parties: a reception for family and friends and a luncheon for just family. Ülle showed up at both. My aunts and uncles loved her light Estonian accent. After the wedding, she danced and laughed with my mother and grandmother. Ülle Lewes taught me English in college, but she taught and still teaches me so much more. Perhaps more than an English professor, she is a life coach. I asked her once about her teaching philosophy, and after a long silence she said, "Challenge them [students] to be better than they think they can be."

Leaving the nurturing tutelage of Ülle at Ohio Wesleyan reminded me of what it felt like to break that childhood connection to my mother. Clarice had molded me and guided me, been there to fight my battles and level her expectations. I still carried a lot of baggage, emotional and otherwise, but we had gotten me this far by faith. But now I was heading into adulthood. Clearly not ready to stand all alone, I would need the counsel and support and mentorship of countless friends and colleagues. Many of them shared those characteristics of passion, toughness, and commitment that my mother and Ülle had. They all would have a pivotal role in shaping my future. But I was no longer simply a student of those around me; it was time to venture out. Apply the lessons learned. Fall and get up again on my own. Though fear and anger were still vital, a spiritual strength and optimism were growing inside me.

EIGHT

Never Say I'll Try, Say I Will

Let not your heart be troubled, neither let it be afraid.

—John 14:27

Where the spirit of the Lord is, there is peace; where the Spirit of the Lord is, there is love.

—Stephen R. Adams

Even while I was knee-deep in my struggles with college academics and working to overcome my stuttering, my mind and heart were growing in focus on a career in broadcast journalism. And why not? My love for words was a result of my struggles with literacy. I believed some good, a new strength, would also come from my difficulties with speech. Much more than belief in my own abilities, it was a belief in God's power. Thus, despite my shortcomings, I never doubted my chosen path. My faith teaches me that there are no obstacles, that all stumbling blocks are merely stepping stones and part of God's plan. It was my responsibility to remain faithful and see what God had in store on the other side of my difficulties.

When I left high school, having moved from functional

illiteracy to a solid transcript, I approached college with relative confidence and the assumption that I was prepared for whatever might come my way. The first year of college was like a blast of frigid air to my psyche. If there had been a basement class, at least one professor we know would have put me there. I was at the bottom looking up again.

Could read but couldn't read fast enough or smart enough.

Could write but my thoughts were a jumbled mess.

Could speak but couldn't speak clearly under pressure.

Knew words but didn't have a wide enough vocabulary.

Yet I was not the same kid I had been at age thirteen. That young Byron was frightened, ashamed, and angry. The older Byron was still angry but beginning to realize that there would always be hurdles. There might always be a period of starting over. I just needed to be patient and faithful and tough enough to work my way to the other side. Admit what I didn't know and ask for help when I needed it, but mostly roll up my sleeves and outwork those around me.

By my senior year at Ohio Wesleyan I was on pretty solid academic ground. I had decided to major in journalism and speech communications, with a minor in political science. Active in sports and school organizations, I had a column for the school newspaper, was news director for the school's cable television news show, co-hosted a nighttime radio show, and worked as a freelance reporter for the local area radio station. It was a big deal for me when I made the regional Associated Press with a story I wrote on a local city council meeting. I stayed up half the night to see my byline cross the wire. I was named one of the top three students in the journalism department based on academic achievement and contributions to the department. We all dreamed of big careers in newspapers or television, becoming the next Bob Woodward or Walter Cronkite. My hero was Ed Bradley. I knew his level of coolness would always elude me, but just maybe his caliber of work might someday be achievable. It was another Pitts family philosophy. Never say you'll try. Say you will. I was raised to believe that if you speak your dreams long enough and loud enough, eventually others will dream and speak with you.

My inspiration to pursue journalism had deep roots. First, there were my struggles with literacy and speech. I took those as signs from God that communication would play a major part in my life. I had convinced myself through Scriptures like Romans 12:21, "Be not overcome of evil, but overcome evil with good," that all the bad things in life had some good purpose if only I searched long enough. So I concluded that journalism was my purpose. In addition to commanding respect, journalists have a significant and valid place in our democracy. As a child, I attended any number of rallies related to social justice and civil rights or big events at my church. I always sat in amazement when the media would show up. The police would behave one way when cameras and reporters were present, often less aggressively. Journalists held the authorities accountable, and that appealed to me. In the days after Dr. Martin Luther King Jr. was assassinated in 1968, there were riots in cities across the country, including Baltimore. On our street, looters vandalized cars that failed to have a black cloth tied to the antenna. Police took that same black cloth as a sign the car belonged to some kind of troublemaker. My father and brother stayed up most of the night, running back and forth to the car to put up or pull down the black cloth, depending on whether there were police or looters on our block. The police were not as violent but they were certainly as aggressive as the looters. One evening, as the police made their way through our neighborhood (there was a police station just a few blocks away), pushing and shoving men and women on the street, a local television crew pulled up. Suddenly, the nightsticks were not being used as aggressively. That moment left an indelible impression on me. Journalists, simply by their presence, could keep the police honest. I wasn't so much bitten by the bug as saw that the bug had teeth.

Why would someone with a history of stuttering choose a career in television? Why not become a print journalist? There were a number of factors. I was a television junkie, having spent hours and hours watching television as a child, especially when the tension in my house was at its highest. Television also kept me company when I was home by myself. Much of what I knew about the world, I learned from television. When it came to gathering news, I was much more comfortable speaking to someone in person as part of a television crew rather than on the telephone, where my stuttering problems might be more apparent. Face-to-face, I could smile or even use my hands for emphasis. I was also a great listener. One of the things I learned in broadcast journalism was to allow the interview subject to fill the silence. That part was easy for me. But I knew I would need practice to overcome my lingering communication issues. I still spoke slowly and deliberately, using the sing-song style I had learned from Dr. Robinson. So I practiced being a television reporter in my dormitory bathroom with a glass and my toothbrush. The top of a glass is about the size of a television camera lens. A toothbrush doesn't resemble a microphone at all, but it's what I had. With a Magic Marker, I traced the edge of the glass on the bathroom mirror, and every morning before class and every night before bed I put on my own mini-newscast. Silly, I know, but since my early struggles with literacy and speech, repetition and routine are things I rely on. The bathroom routine was about practicing the mechanics of television news.

My decision to pursue a career in journalism was solidified after hearing the stories of the guest lecturers who appeared on campus during my time at OWU, such as investigative reporter Jack Anderson and network television correspondent Emery King. In the 1980s, King was one of a handful of African-American television network news correspondents. He served NBC News as its White House correspondent covering the Reagan administration, and later spent nineteen years as an anchor in Detroit. During my senior year King spoke at OWU as part of a university lecture series. He spoke of the highs and lows of broadcast journalism as well as his travels around the globe. I had the honor of picking him up at the airport with a few of my classmates. As was my pattern back then, I was still very shy about speaking in unfamiliar settings, without the opportunity to rehearse and with people who might sense my limitations and dismiss me. So I said very little in his presence. Too nervous, anxious about my stutter, and, frankly, convinced I had nothing worth saying, I certainly made no impression on the man.

But a notable thing happened after his lecture as we were walking him back to the car. One of my female classmates stopped him on the stairwell and said, "Mr. King, thank you for talking to us. We will always remember what you said."

Now here's the line that made Emery King stop in his tracks. "But I want you to remember one name," she said. "Byron Pitts. He will be at the network someday."

King seemed surprised by my classmate's bold prediction. I was stunned. Perhaps I had spoken my ambitious plan aloud so often people around me were beginning to believe it. My friend's words were powerful because it was the first time I had heard anyone, not even my mother to this point, affirm out loud what my career goals were. It was like a needle full of adrenaline in the heart. For years I had quietly claimed my future career as a network journalist, and now others were claiming it with me. Emery King politely smiled and got in his car. Years later I met him on assignment. He didn't recall the moment, nor did he have any real reason to. But I will always remember it. I have never stopped affirming (or claiming) what I want, and I have always found support from those who join me. It is amazing how you can transform a dream into a reality by saying it until you believe it and others believe it with you. It can become a call to arms. You say it. You believe it. You then devote your dreams and your sweat to it.

That May the dream of my mother, my grandmother, Dr. Lewes, and countless supporters back in East Baltimore came to pass. I put on a cap and gown and joined the 1982 graduating class of Ohio Wesleyan. I was grateful to be graduating on time. I remember the pride stitched across the faces of my family. My mother, brother, sister, and grandmother were in attendance. Remember we are not a big smiling family, but I did see a few teeth that day. It was a bittersweet day for me. I was not focused so much on what I had accomplished or where I was headed as on the people I was about to leave behind. I had grown close to people like Dr. Lewes, my friend Pete, and others. Those kinds of emotional separations had always been tough for me since the breakup of my parents' marriage.

As I left the stage with my degree in hand, I paused so my brother could take a picture. Since no one in my family could snap a good photograph before there was automatic focus, we had albums full of blurry memories. In the age of digital cameras, none of us have managed to frame very well. Today we have crisp family photos with little head room or odd angles.

After my brother snapped his picture, I handed my degree to my mother. "You worked as hard as I did," I whispered to her. "You deserve this more than me."

She hugged me to the point of discomfort, kissed my cheek, and handed my degree back to me. "God worked harder than either of us. This is His, but you hold on to it in the meantime," she said, with the corners of her mouth nearly touching her ears. We laughed. I walked back to my seat with my wrinkled robe blowing in the breeze. I was actually a bit sad when the day was done. I have always enjoyed the journey more than the destination.

That was a Saturday. The following Monday I started work at *The Carolinian* newspaper in Raleigh, North Carolina, where my mom had relocated a few years earlier. It was a weekly newspaper published by a local African-American businessman and aimed at an African-American audience. As a reporter, photographer, sportswriter, copy editor, and go-get-the-boss-cigarettes-when-he-called-for-them, I was paid handsomely: one hundred dollars every Friday, five twenty-dollar bills in a small brown envelope. I assumed the envelope was small so the rolled-up twenties would seem like a larger sum of money. It was modest pay for joyous work. Despite the minimal sum, I was now a working journalist. My mother was simply thrilled I had a job she could describe to her siblings in one sentence. "Byron is a reporter in Raleigh," she'd say. To hear her brag to her friends and family, it was as if I was a staff writer for *The New York Times*.

There were countless lessons to learn at *The Carolinian*. It was all hands on deck for every issue. I reported on everything from city government to sporting events to obituaries. And I covered a lot of crime. But included in those lessons was humility. It was tough showing up at those first few news conferences with a Polaroid camera, lined paper instead of a reporter's notebook, and a pen donated by a local funeral parlor. We weren't issued business cards, so my mother printed some for me on a copy machine at her job. Thus, my career in journalism started like most new phases of my life: modestly. There was only one way to look and that was up. I was not setting the world on fire, but I showed up on time, stayed late, and did whatever the boss asked of me, usually with a smile on my face. On its worst day, being at *The Carolinian* beat cutting grass on Interstate 95 in the summer.

Even though I lived at home with my mother, it was hard to stretch a hundred dollars a week very far. After four months at the newspaper, I reluctantly took a job at Shaw University in Raleigh as sports information director. It was a better-paying position but offered more shots of humility without a chaser. I was no closer to my dream of being a broadcast journalist and was concerned that I was, in fact, moving away from that career. I wanted to be a hard newsman, not some glad-handing public relations flak. My mother, who knew I was disappointed with my career moves thus far, and who had always found solutions in the past, had the idea that I should meet more people in the broadcast profession. When she once found out there was going to be a nationally televised college basketball tournament in town, with one of the legendary voices of sports radio attending, she encouraged me: "You should meet him. I bet he'd help you."

We got tickets to the tournament just to meet this famed sportscaster. I can't imagine the tickets were very expensive, but I am certain it was money for which we could have found some other use. Standing high in the stands (the cheap seats), my mother spotted the sportscaster down on the floor. "There he is, baby! Let's go meet him," she said with schoolgirl excitement. This was not a request. She had already pulled me out of my seat and we were heading downstairs. "Momma, can we at least wait until halftime? He looks busy right now," I said, with the embarrassment of a twenty-two-year-old being dragged by his mother, pained by every step.

"Well then, let's get close to him. He's a busy man, I'm sure." Clarice is nothing if not persistent. Keep in mind this is the woman who rarely smiles. On this occasion, you could count her teeth from the other side of the arena as she stood patiently for halftime and her moment to introduce her son to the sportscaster she was convinced would change her child's life.

The halftime buzzer rang, and Clarice made a beeline for the press desk. "Hello, sir. My name is Clarice Pitts. I'm a big fan of yours. This is my son, Byron. He just graduated from Ohio Wesleyan University with a degree in journalism. He wants a career in journalism. Could you offer him any advice?" she asked, with a degree of desperation I rarely ever heard in my mother's voice.

The sportscaster never took her outstretched hand. He barely looked away from his notes. He did size me up for a moment, cleared his throat, and said, "You should probably do something else. Broadcasting is a tough business." End of sentence. We were wasting his time. He stood up and brushed my mother's shoulder as he walked away. I wanted to kick his ass right there. Just jump on him and beat him until he learned common courtesy.

Finally, my mother lowered her hand, her smile painfully

melted away. "Let that be a lesson to you, son. When you make it, never act that way. I guess God didn't want us talking to him after all," she said as she pulled at my arm again, this time headed back up to the bleachers.

I still wanted to kick his ass. That thought may seem like an overreaction, and perhaps it was, but that moment took me back to my childhood. How many times had I watched some person in authority treat my mother disrespectfully? From store clerks, to bosses, to a construction worker on a street corner or one of the many therapists we met when I was in grade school. How many times had I been bullied in school or on the way to school?

I believe there are assumptions that some people in positions of power or influence make about those on the other side. As a boy, I was too small, too weak, and too frightened to stand up to their slights, but I was no less offended by them. All those moments from the past pressed on my shoulders, like a tight lid on a boiling pot, and often sent me into a rage whenever someone was less than respectful of my mother or any person they viewed as vulnerable. Without question, those feelings existed deep in the dark places of my heart. But I used them like fuel. I was keeping score. It always kept me pressing forward to prove myself or defend others.

Years later, after I had joined *CBS News* as a correspondent, I ran into this famed sports broadcaster again. We were both covering the Super Bowl in Miami. My credentials gave wider access to the field and to players. There's that old saying about revenge being best served cold. I have never sought revenge, never rubbed a slight in anyone's face, but I have always made a mental note.

"Byron, you do a great job. I watch you all the time," he said with a bright smile during our sideline encounter.

"Thank you, sir, awfully kind of you to say," I replied with a firm handshake. "My mother is a big fan of yours," I added, thinking the whole time I would kill him with kindness, though deep down I wanted to punch that smile off his face. To this day, his behavior toward my mother is one of the reasons I do my best to give as much time as possible to anyone who asks. Every college student and fledgling reporter gets my full attention and a few minutes of my time. I don't want to dampen anyone else's dream the way that sportscaster made me feel.

In many ways, working at Shaw was like a postgraduate year after college. Shaw is one of the nation's historically black colleges. It had a compact, friendly campus like Ohio Wesleyan. In addition to working at Shaw, I returned to WTVD, Raleigh's ABC affiliate, where I had interned during my junior year in college. I would work days at Shaw, writing press releases and logging sports scores, then I would spend my nights, unpaid, at WTVD pulling scripts for the eleven o'clock late news. During these days before computers, TV anchors read from typed scripts that entry-level staffers and interns manually loaded into the teleprompter. Although this was not hard-news reporting, it was a chance to keep a toe in the business. It also gave me the opportunity to reunite with my old friend Larry Stogner, my original mentor and a reporter's reporter.

When I first met Larry, he scared me to death. Looking more like a banker than a reporter, he always wore a white shirt and a suit and tie, and was almost always deadly serious. He was a chain-smoker with a demeanor as hard as the briefcase he seemed to carry everywhere. He had one of those TV voices that revealed decades of smoking unfiltered cigarettes and drinking coffee. He was probably in his thirties when we worked together, but Larry carried himself like a guy who had been on earth a very long time. He was the station's go-to guy, and as best I could tell, most of the other reporters and anchors on staff feared and respected him.

The night before my first day as an intern, I had gone to the local library and read back issues of the hometown newspaper, *The Raleigh News and Observer*. I wanted to at least sound like I knew something about the news. That morning my mother made me breakfast, we said a long prayer, and she dropped me off on her way to work.

"God bless you, son," she said as she drove away. We hardly ever wished each other luck, since there wasn't much in life we ever attributed to luck. With a full stomach, a head full of newspaper clippings and Bible verses read at home, and at least one verse typed on an index card and placed in my sports coat that morning by my mother, I walked into the Raleigh newsroom ready to conquer the world.

"You're late" is how Larry greeted me that first day.

"Good morning, sir. I was told to report here by nine o'clock. It's not nine yet," I said with a tone of confidence in my voice.

"Chickenshit reporters may get in at nine, but I get here at eight, and I expect my intern here when I get here," Larry said, with his feet on his desk, a cup of coffee in his hand, a cigarette in his mouth, and both eyes on the morning paper. "You don't want to be some chickenshit reporter, do you?" he said, as he glanced up from his paper.

"No, sir. Good morning, Mr. Stogner. I'm Byron Pitts," I said. My morning confidence left by the door, I was now in a puddle of sweat.

"Well, good. We all work hard in this bureau, and we are all serious about the news. You serious about the news, son, or do you want to be some chickenshit anchor someday?" he said.

"No, sir, I want to be a newsman," I answered, confidence creeping back up my spine.

"Then good, every good newsman knows how to make coffee. Coffee machine is in the back room. Get to it," he said in what would be our lengthiest conversation of the day. Perhaps I wasn't the fastest learner he had ever had in the office, but Larry seemed to take a liking to me. Within a few days I graduated from making the coffee in the morning to picking up Larry's cigarettes. Years of going to the store to pick up my mother's cigarettes were finally paying off.

"Wear a sports coat tomorrow. We're going to the state house," Larry yelled as I walked out of the office at the end of a shift.

That was Larry's style, similar to my mother: do what I say and we'll get along fine. And we did. It was one of the best summers of my life; the state house one day, a murder scene the next, and I had a front-row seat with one of the finest reporters in North Carolina. Actually, it was more like a back seat, crunched between camera equipment and old bags of fast food, but I felt like Edward R. Murrow or Ed

Bradley in the back of that news truck. Larry usually worked with a young cameraman named Eddie Barber. While I never saw Larry without a shirt and tie, I assumed Eddie didn't own one. A total free spirit, he was always smiling, always upbeat, and always willing to go anywhere to tell a story with his camera. He was a wonderful example of always having a good attitude. No matter how lousy the assignment or how foul Larry's mood, Eddie was always enthusiastically at his side. He was also a great encourager. He patiently listened to my dreams about a career in television and would end every conversation with the same words of encouragement: "Go for it."

While Larry was a father figure, Eddie was like an older brother. Larry and Eddie never seemed to care about the color of my skin. They worked hard and seemed to appreciate my desire to do the same. To the bosses and staff at the main building in Durham, they were the odd couple. They taught me some valuable lessons, including, Never judge a person by what you see on the outside. On the outside, the three of us had next to nothing in common, and they certainly had no reason to take any interest in me. But they did. When Eddie would get a call about a murder overnight, he'd give me a call and swing by my mother's house to pick me up, just so I could get some experience. And Larry protected me from the sometimes unpleasant realities of the language and biases in the newsroom. Like the time we went to a murder scene "in the ghetto," as someone in the newsroom described it on the car radio. "Those people are animals, so you boys better be careful." Turned out the crime scene was less than a block from my mother's home.

Larry could see the hurt in my eyes as he glanced back at me through the rearview mirror. "Don't be an idiot," he barked back into the radio. I met Larry's smile with a smile of my own. He winked at me and said, "Son, don't ever let idiots bother you." His advice has served me well my entire career.

Now, two years later, I was back in the WTVD newsroom, for a free stint after college. Larry was no longer interested in having me make his coffee. "You weren't very good at it," he later confessed. "We got to get you a job," he said. And he did. It was my first lesson in the age-old saying, "It's not always what you know, it sometimes helps who you know and who you stay in contact with."

How fortunate I was to stay in contact with Larry Stogner. Without any professional advice or support like Larry's, when I graduated from college I had sent out more than forty videocassettes with samples of my writing and on-camera work to small television stations across the country. Places like Toledo, Savannah, Jackson, Mississippi, and Cedar Rapids, Iowa. About a dozen news managers were kind enough to write back. Most were form letters. One was handwritten. They all said the same thing: Thanks but no thanks. One news director at a small station in eastern North Carolina was a friend of cameraman Eddie Barber. Eddie called to see if the news director had received my tape.

"Yep, got it," he told Eddie. "Tell your friend he's wasting his time. I see a lot of tapes. He doesn't have what it takes. He's wasting his time." I guess it was his idea of doing me or Eddie a favor.

Eddie's response to me was "Don't worry about him. Just

keep going for it." As fate would have it, sixteen months later this same news director at this same station in eastern North Carolina had a job opening. Eddie encouraged me to apply again.

"He hated my work before. Why would he like it now? I don't have a new tape," I insisted.

"Just go for it," Eddie said. "And have Larry call the guy."

With the same tape and a recommendation from Larry Stogner, I applied again. Oddly enough, the news director seemed thrilled to get a personal phone call from a big-name reporter in Raleigh.

"I love this kid's tape. If you vouch for him, that's good enough for me," he said to Larry. He never interviewed me, but he did give me the job. By the time I started, he'd been fired. Had I missed my chance to kill him with kindness? Not exactly. We met years later. It was a familiar reunion: "Byron, nice to meet you. I'm a big fan of your work." He clearly had no recollection of the actual role he had once played in my career.

"Good to meet you, sir," I said with a smile and another insincere but firm handshake.

I started at WNCT-TV in Greenville, North Carolina, as a general assignment reporter and weekend sports anchor for an annual salary of $8,600. I was thrilled. My mother was angry. I had been earning about $20,000 at Shaw with a small expense account and an assistant.

"It's okay to dream, son, but don't be dumb about it" was my mother's response to the news that I was moving out of her house to take my first paying job in broadcast news.

Oh, by the way, I could no longer afford my own car. It just meant I would have to live within walking distance of my first job in television.

"Your tuition was more than they're paying you. Are you sure you want to take a step back like that?" she asked.

Two steps forward, one step back. That's how it had always been. When I left for Greenville, my mother wasn't speaking to me. We did not talk for a few weeks. Now that I was out of college, there would be no more letters written in red ink. Mother would express her disapproval from then on with deafening silence.

My first news director was a guy named Roy Hardee. He was a forty-something news manager who had cut his teeth on Southern newspapers and Southern radio. He preferred penny loafers, button-down shirts, his weekly crewcut, and pork barbecue for lunch. He knew more cops by their first names and their favorite beverage than any other newsperson I have ever known. Roy was always suspicious of reporters more focused on polishing their résumés than on covering local news. Thus, he greeted most new (and most often from the North) reporters the same way. Using both hands to hitch up his pants, just before he sucked his teeth, he said, "So you think you can cover the news?" It always came across as less of a question and more of a threat.

Because it was a small station with a small budget, most people were hired to do more than one job. I was a weekday news reporter and weekend sports anchor. It looked good on the business card, but it was a tough way to make a living. I lived in a one-bedroom apartment with at least one roommate, and for a brief time two. We learned the finer points of macaroni and cheese, tuna fish, and on rare occasions grilled chicken. Since we were paid so little at work and were constantly hungry, searching out free meals was sometimes a motivation for covering stories. One way the staff would decide which press conference we would attend on any given day depended on which organization provided the best food. The East Carolina University football coach's weekly press conference was always a favorite: sandwiches and shrimp cocktail.

That was the best part of being a sports reporter. I was eating with the best sportscasters in the state. Unfortunately, when it came to actually being a sportscaster, I was, to put it gently, awful. I had assumed (there's that word again), since I had played high school and college football, had been around athletes and coaches all my life, that being a sportscaster would be easy. Wrong! You actually have to know something about all sports. I never liked or even understood soccer until my children played many years later, and I thought tennis was a sport you played to pick up girls.

Needless to say, my career as a sportscaster did not last very long. But it lasted long enough for me to discover that I loved news reporting. I was allowed to change beats. I became what was known at the time as a one-man band. I was the reporter, photographer, producer, and editor wrapped in one. The station gave me a big van with the station call letters on the side. Fortunately, since there were no side windows on my van, no one ever knew the only thing inside the manual-shift vehicle was a video camera, a few tapes, extra batteries, and a spare tire. It wasn't much to look at, but it was all the gear I was responsible for, and now my dream had a starting point: I was a television reporter.

My beat was the small town of Washington, North Carolina, affectionately known as Little Washington, with a population under ten thousand. I would spend my day between the courthouse and the jail. I pretended to be Larry Stogner: white shirt, tie, and a sports coat. Who could afford a suit on less than nine thousand a year? Only a breath ahead of the Carolinian newspaper in Raleigh, we occasionally had real notebooks. I no longer carried pens engraved with the name and address of the local mortician. I had upgraded to the local gas station pens or the ones I could swipe from the sales department. I also learned that napkins and fast-food lunch bags make for wonderful writing surfaces in a pinch. I was in heaven.

Reporting for television is not particularly an art form or a science as much as it is a craft. WNCT-TV in Greenville was my first apprenticeship, a place to learn the very basics. In athletics, there are people who have been described as naturals. The same is true in broadcast communication. I have had colleagues over the years who seemed as if they were born to be on television. For them, talking on television is as simple as inhaling. Nothing about broadcasting ever came easy to me. What I have learned to do, even the simplest things, I have learned through practice. One of the first things I worked on in Greenville was the proper way to hold a microphone. That may sound ridiculous, but consider this: John Wooden, one of the most successful college basketball coaches of all time, insisted on teaching his players the proper way to put on their socks. No detail is too small to practice. Because of my long thin fingers, there wasn't a natural way for me to look manly holding a microphone. Do I hold it in my fist? What about three fingers, as if it's a flute? Do I hold it directly under my chin or off to the side? That's how I spent many evenings at home in Greenville, North Carolina, working on the best way to hold a microphone. Is it more effective to stand directly in front of a speaker at a news conference or off to the side? After some practice, I decided it was better to stand off to one side. The person would have to physically turn his head in order to face you. It proved easier to sneak in a quick followup question once you had the person's attention, and it seemed easier to turn away from a questioner directly in front. As a one-man-band photographer/reporter in Greenville, I would practice setting up in different spots at news conferences. It was a game I'd play. I kept notes on where the speaker would look first to answer questions. Which side would they look to most often? Through trial and error, I discovered it was often better to start the question—if I was competing for attention—with the person's name. Make everything as personal as possible.

Once, for example, while covering a murder trial in Little Washington, I got to know the families of a victim and of the accused killer. Every morning before trial and at the end of the day cameramen and reporters would run outside the courthouse and yell questions at the accused. He would always just look straight ahead. During one recess, I was talking to his mother. She called the man by his nickname. Relatives called him Junior. I held on to that small bit of information until the man was convicted and sentenced to die. That day at the end of court I waited by the police car. Reporters yelled their familiar questions. No response. As he approached in leg irons, with my camera on my shoulder and my microphone in hand,

I had one chance, "Hey, Junior! You ready to die?" The man stopped and turned to the voice that had called his name; we made eye contact. "I don't want to die. What I did was wrong, but I don't want to die." He looked scared. After days of sitting in court acting like a tough guy, this convicted killer finally showed a glimpse of fear. That night I got a "way to go" from Roy Hardee. But, more important, I got a call at the station from the victim's family. They were glad to see the killer had finally shown some emotion. The lesson for me that day was to always look for some human connection, whether to saints or sinners.

For all that I learned in Greenville as a hungry young reporter, I probably lost about fifteen pounds. Call it the price of an education. The first time I went home to Baltimore to visit, I ran into my high school buddy, Joe Stumbroski.

"Hey, Byron, you've lost so much weight. I heard you were in television. Are you a model?" Joe asked innocently.

"Nah, man, I'm starting in the basement. Call it remedial reading for reporters," I answered without a hint of regret. We both smiled.

All I had ever prayed for was a chance. God was giving me that chance. By this time I had an army of family and friends praying for me and pulling for me. Greenville was a long way from East Baltimore or Ohio Wesleyan, for that matter. But I wasn't alone. I never had been. I was not just trying my hand in television. I was doing it. I am sure I didn't strike the most impressive pose as a young reporter: Razor-thin, big Afro, big glasses, high-pitched voice, the three shirts I owned all worn around the collar. I looked more like a backup singer for the Commodores hooked on crack than a credible reporter. But based on where I started? Faith had carried me this far, so I just kept my head up, pushed my shoulders back, and kept stepping out on nothing. What a glorious ride. Next stop, Norfolk.

NINE

It Never Gets Easier—You Just Get Stronger

Consider it pure joy, my brothers, whenever you face trials of many kinds, because you know that the testing of your faith develops perseverance. Perseverance must finish its work so that you may be mature and complete, not lacking anything.

—James 1:2–4

WHERE'S THE BEER?" PHIL Smith was holding the door to my refrigerator open, staring at its contents, which consisted of a single large plastic jug of sweet tea, a carton of eggs, and a well-used bottle of Tabasco sauce.

"I don't drink," I said.

Standing six feet six and north of 250 pounds, Phil looked around with a disgusted look on his face. "You are such a loser," he said. Everyone in the room laughed.

It was Norfolk, Virginia, 1984. I had invited several friends from my new job at television station WAVY-TV over to my apartment for pizza and a college football bowl game. We were all young and single and working jobs we loved in a great city. It was a collegial group. Since many of us had begun our television careers in smaller markets, like my experience in Greenville, Norfolk was a step into big-city news. After an intense week, the favorite wind-down activity was a night of conversation about work, listening to music, dancing, lots of laughter, and alcohol. I was not a drinker and never learned to dance, so I was often the odd man out on those occasions. This particular night, it became clear just how different I really was. After the football game was over, one of my friends suggested that we watch a movie. They started going through my pile of VHS tapes next to the television. Much to their surprise, every single tape in the stack was a recording of a network newscast.

My closest friend in the group shook his head and announced, "You really are a loser." Even I laughed this time.

Back in college, that's the way many friends would affectionately label me at parties—a loser. "He doesn't drink, and he can't dance" was how many male friends would introduce me to their female friends. To which I would respond, "But I will graduate on time." By my early twenties, being considered an outsider was a badge of honor. I was used to it, almost preferred it that way. For the longest time I had always felt that it was God, Clarice, and me against the world. Now that I lived in a different city, mostly it was just God and me, and God was doing all the heavy lifting. That is one big reason why I have often been alone but never lonely.

My faith was just one of the things that made me feel different from my colleagues. There were professional differences as well. The goal of many reporters is to be the station's next anchorman or anchorwoman. Not me. I wanted to be a reporter, eventually at the network level, and knew that it was going to take a singleminded focus to become the best in the business. I didn't really make time for distractions. Many of my colleagues had wide-ranging interests. One reporter loved riding his motorcycle. Another talked about his love for surfing. Another had a great wine collection. I arrived in Norfolk with a couch, a card table, two chairs, a television set, and a VCR that I used to record the *CBS Evening News*, *ABC's World News Tonight*, and the *NBC Nightly News*. Many thought my focus was too narrow, but childhood difficulties had taught me to keep things simple and linear. Through every obstacle, the keys to success for me have always been the same: prayer, grace, structure, hard work, and more prayer. Whenever I have succeeded, it was because I stuck to the plan. Whenever I have failed, it has usually occurred because I deviated from the plan. There was very little time in my life for distractions.

The move to a bigger market was going to mean greater scrutiny of my performance and greater expectations for the quality of work. In Greenville, my slow, deliberate process had not been a liability. Since I had been expected to deliver one complete report each day, I generally had time to write several drafts of my script until I was satisfied with the product. But in Norfolk I had to report at least two and sometimes three stories a day. This requirement exposed a process that I had managed to keep hidden. When I first learned to read, I read everything out loud. When I began to write my news scripts, I would "write out loud," reading to myself as I put the words on paper. In Greenville, because I worked alone, my process had never been seen or heard by anyone else. In Norfolk, I was now regularly teamed up with a cameraman, who was with me nearly all the time, and we had to work on much tighter deadlines. I felt self-conscious and uncomfortable. When I began to speak on my side of the van, at least one cameraman would turn up the radio in annoyance. But some seemed more amused by my process. "You know that's weird, don't you?" asked one photographer, Tom Costanza. Tom and I were often teamed together. He was on the short list of those who didn't mind my chatter in the news vehicle. "I get why you talk out loud while you write," Tom said, while we were out on another story, "but have you ever thought about whispering?" Maybe he was on to something.

While I continued to work on the mechanics of the broadcast craft, how best to hold a microphone or position myself at a press conference, the one natural talent I brought to my profession was the ability to understand the thread of humanity in every news story and find a way for the viewer to connect and relate. Most news stories are stories about struggle: a struggle for political or economic power, a struggle over land, a struggle over life and death. More than who wins or loses, I relate most to the struggle. Most of the reporters in Norfolk had more experience than me, better contacts, were better writers, and many had wonderful voices. But I decided that no one had an intrinsic understanding of struggle and could bring that experience to life as I could. Take what little you have and build on it. That was something Father Bart had taught me back in high school at Archbishop Curley. It doesn't matter where you start, only where you finish. I came to Norfolk with few material possessions and limited ability, but what I did possess I could build upon with God's grace. That was all I could do. And just as in the past, it would have to be enough. As a young general-assignment reporter, I had to learn in a hurry how to make those connections on a story.

One of my first such experiences in Norfolk was a fatal car crash that killed five young men in November of 1985, members of a basketball team driving home from a tournament. The accident had occurred over the weekend. I was assigned to the story with one of the best photographers at the station, Michael Ridge. There was no video of the accident scene, and the authorities would not allow us to take pictures of the damaged cars. None of the relatives wanted to talk on camera. It appeared that the opportunity to tell an important story in a compelling way might be lost. But we did not give up. We eventually convinced the grieving families to provide us with pictures of the five young men. At the home of one family, Michael persuaded those assembled to let us photograph the pictures on the kitchen table. Being in the house reminded me of the many times I had been in the home of relatives during the first few days of mourning. Some people wanted to be left alone. Some needed to talk.

These five families were no different from mine. I had found a human connection. We politely asked if anyone who wanted to say something in remembrance of the five young men would come into the kitchen, in front of the photo array, in front of our microphone, and just talk. We did not ask any questions. We just listened. A few of the mourners welcomed the opportunity. Ranging in age from late teens to early twenties, most of the five were lifelong friends. They went to the same church. Some were in college. One elderly man with a deep scratchy voice said something that has always stuck with me. He said, "Death is something you never get used to." The comment was simple yet profound. Like almost every other family in a similar situation, these families would survive what happened, but they would never get used to it.

That night we aired our story on the accident, using family photographs, the voices of relatives, and video from the highway. One of the anchors choked up on the air. Colleagues who had never spoken to me before complimented me on the piece. And some of the relatives called after the broadcast to thank us for honoring their loved ones respectfully. We had captured and communicated a human moment.

Despite some success early on, I still felt like a country bumpkin in the big city in Norfolk. Compared to Greenville it was a high-rise metropolis. I was not one of those twenty-something reporters who was full of myself, believing I could conquer the world or that I was ready for big-time television. I was a kid who simply believed I had the tools to work hard and make up for my shortcomings as a reporter. I was full of energy but not confidence.

Terrell Harris was a reporter at the ABC affiliate who covered the same beat. He was everything I wasn't—good-looking and confident, he wore expensive suits and drove a fancy car. All the girls in Norfolk seemed to be in love with him. I owned two blazers, three pair of slacks, two red ties, one yellow tie, two pairs of brown loafers, and one shirt collar extender. I walked to work. Every time I saw him on a story I felt intimidated.

In fact, the only time I have ever stuttered on the air was during a live shot, when I was standing next to Terrell Harris. We were both covering a case of government corruption in the county. We were lined up outside the government office doing our live shots for the noon news on our respective stations. My trick to avoid stuttering in general on the air—but particularly on live shots—was to carefully prepare and rehearse what I intended to say. I needed that repetition to ensure that I would say every word correctly. A few minutes before noon I was rehearsed and ready. But that morning it had been snowing, which was unusual for Norfolk, and rather than hearing the introduction I expected on the corruption story, the anchor asked me a question about the weather. I froze. I was unable to react quickly to the unexpected question. In trying to respond, I stuttered. I intended to say that it had started to snow when we first arrived this morning. But it came out as "s-s-s-s-s-s-snow." I looked at my feet to try to kick-start my brain. I saw the cameraman peek from behind his camera in amazement, and I could hear Terrell next to me delivering his live report flawlessly. I wanted to die. To my relief, the cameraman kindly moved the camera away from my face to take pictures of the snow. It gave me a moment to gather my thoughts. I produced a nervous smile, imagined I could see my grandmother's face (which calmed me down), and got back on the topic I was prepared to discuss.

That night I ate my dinner alone in an edit suite and watched that live shot over and over again. I made a copy on a VHS tape and took it home so I could watch it again. I wanted to study it to see if there was a way to prevent something like that from ever happening again. But the shame has never left me.

I went to every story thinking every other reporter was

smarter than me, knew more than me, and had more talent. I tended to fight my sense of insecurity by getting angry, and in my mind Terrell was the standard I needed to beat. I would purposely take offense at the smallest slight. If the police chief answered his question first, I would get angry. If he got more time for his story than I got for mine, I would get angry. But rather than raise my voice or force a confrontation, I used the anger as motivation to improve my performance. Because it often took me a bit more time to read through the press releases or the prep material, I had to apply a different set of skills to my work. Thus, if my competitor interviewed two people, I would interview four. I would always have to do my best to get to the story first. I would also have to make sure I left the story last to pick up any crumbs the other reporters had left behind. Like Terrell, I needed to develop some techniques for nurturing sources. Terrell was tight with all the secretaries in city hall and the police headquarters, so I worked the people in the maintenance department. Terrell knew the hot spots in town and could meet sources after hours, and I would just hang out at the police station at night with the people forced to work the night shift. Terrell had his ways, and I found mine.

At my station, there was a reporter named Ed Hazelwood. With a thick beard, glasses, and a deep baritone voice, Ed won numerous awards for his investigative work and for any number of reports on the U.S. military. But that's not what impressed me most about him. It was the notebook he kept with the names and numbers of every contact he ever made. He had them listed by title, profession, spouse's name, their girlfriend's phone number, and address if needed. His contacts were always at his fingertips. He'd call people just to check in. He called contacts on their birthdays, their children's birthday, a bar mitzvah, any special occasion, or just to say hello. In a business where we are often takers showing up at the doorstep in the midst of some personal tragedy, Ed was a giver. He respected the people with whom he came in contact. But that's not to say they were always thrilled to hear from Ed or were pleased with his reporting—just that he respected his contacts.

If Ed kept names and phone numbers and birth dates, so would I. Somewhere along the way, I picked up the idea of sending handwritten notes to people kind enough to give me their time or an interview. It's something I have done for most of my career. "Kindness will take you a long way in this life," my grandmother always used to say. Most people have never written back, but those who have always seemed to appreciate the simple gesture. Besides, a person interviewed today might become a source or an expert the next day, and on a few occasions they have even become a friend. It was one more vital tool for my tool bag, and I knew I needed a good tool bag. I had places to go and things God wanted me to do.

My goal was to make it to the network by age thirty-five. Based on my research, thirty-five was about the median age for a young network correspondent. But my journey required baby steps, or rather two steps forward and one step back. I wanted to become a network correspondent for two basic reasons. For one, it is the biggest stage for a broadcast journalist. That same stubborn child who wanted to read Hemingway now insisted that the most exclusive club in television would someday open its doors to him. The second reason was that it would be the only way my mother and grandmother would ever get to see me regularly on television. From 1982 to 1996, during my career in local news, I changed markets about every two years and worked in cities up and down the eastern seaboard, while my family was mostly based in North Carolina. Occasionally, I would send a videocassette to my mother and grandmother so they could see my work. Somehow, sending them a tape once in a while never seemed to satisfy them. When she did see my work, my grandmother had this sound she would make, like a single grunt, but she would hold it for several seconds, as if it were a song. She would make that sound with a high-pitched voice, and then say, "Baby, you sure look good on my television." No praise from a boss or a television critic ever meant as much as the sound she made and the smile that followed. She would have appreciated seeing me more often.

However, over the years my grandmother did express concern about how often I changed jobs on my way to the network. "What's wrong baby?" she'd say with her Southern drawl. "Why can't you keep a job for very long?" She was talking about my stops in Greenville, Norfolk, Orlando, Tampa, Boston, Atlanta, and Washington, D.C. As I said, I took the long way. I knew I needed a body of work and a wealth of experience to be ready for the network. I didn't want to end up in the revolving door I had seen for other journalists of color at the network level. I kept track of all the network correspondents, and with a few notable exceptions, I noticed what looked like a pattern for African-

Americans who would arrive and then disappear a few years later. When I asked why it happened, I received a variety of explanations, ranging from blatant discrimination to a shortage of opportunities to a lack of preparedness. It depended on whether I was asking a manager or another journalist of color. Since the odds might be against me, I wanted to make sure I was prepared in every possible way. That meant choosing my next jobs with a purpose.

In 1989 I had a chance to work in New York, Chicago, or Boston. I chose Boston, the sixth largest television market in the country. Though it was smaller than New York or Chicago, it was the perfect environment for things I needed to learn. The city had a reputation for producing some of the best writers in journalism, and I knew that one of the criticisms that followed many African-American correspondents at the network was that they couldn't write a good script. I wanted to polish my writing skills, and Boston was the place to do it. This newsroom was the first where my colleagues spent much of their time discussing sentence structure and phraseology.

I quickly learned one important distinction between the smaller markets and the top-ten newsrooms. There was no tolerance for using emotion as a substitute for good reporting. One of my first big stories in Boston was a house fire with fatalities, and I was the only one to secure an interview with a relative of the victims. The woman cried throughout the interview, and I thought I had done an admirable job in capturing the drama of the event. In my previous jobs I would have been praised for such an emotional delivery—but not in Boston. The next morning the news director called me to his office to chastise me for sensationalizing the story and wasting time with a crying interview when I could have been reporting more facts of the story.

In addition to writing, there was another important reason why I chose Boston. Of the three cities where I could have worked, the Boston station had the least diversity in the newsroom, and I wanted to test my skill and my temperament in such a setting. Within weeks of my arrival, I got what I asked for with a major breaking news story. A white man named Charles Stewart accused a black man of shooting and killing his pregnant wife. As the reporter on the night beat, I covered the initial report for our eleven o'clock newscast. By morning, it had morphed into one of the most sensational crime stories in Boston since the Boston Strangler. Stewart's depiction of the attack on his wife was chilling, and his claim that a black man was the perpetrator ignited the undercurrent of racial tension in the city. I was called in early the morning after the shooting to attend a special editorial meeting, where assignments were being handed out and where I happened to be the only African-American in the room. A manager turned to me and said, "We need reaction from the black community. Why don't you go call your contacts?" Since I had been living in the city only for a few weeks, my "contacts" were nonexistent. But his assumption remained: I was black, therefore I had black contacts, and I was to cover the black angle of the story.

I knew I didn't want to be pigeonholed into covering only race, but I wanted to appear to be a team player. My immediate response was "You want my contacts in Tampa?" (my previous station). There was nervous laughter and the realization that the request might have been ill conceived, given my brief tenure in Boston. But I agreed to take on the assignment and pursued it aggressively. Eventually, police uncovered the truth, that Charles Stewart had killed his wife and created a mythical assailant upon whom to place the blame. A year later, in the aftermath of that case, many journalists in Boston's newsrooms were forced to examine how a lack of staff diversity adversely affected the coverage of the Stewart case and how their own biased assumptions about class and race had become part of the coverage.

I will always remember the night a black family had their front door firebombed in one of the city's housing projects. The photographer and I walked up to three elderly white women. "Excuse me, ladies, my name is Byron Pitts. I'm a reporter from Channel 5. What do you think about what happened to one of your neighbors?" I asked. The women looked at me expressionless when one of them said, "We don't want any niggers living here. They should have known better." The photographer I was with turned to me, smiled, and said, "Welcome to Boston." It left an impression. I fought to make my own reporting more reflective of the population we served. For me, it was a challenging time but a growth experience, working in a racially charged environment, learning to keep my cool but not compromising what I believed to be my journalistic or moral integrity. I ended up spending five years in Boston, covering politics and crime, and doing some investigative reporting.

I have been asked plenty of times if racism exists in the news business. The simple answer is that racism and other -isms have always existed in America. Newsrooms are not immune. Like many people in many professions, I have bumped up against the low expectations of others. Whether you are black, white, brown, or yellow, low expectations can weigh you down like an anvil. For one thing, I was often hired as the "black" reporter. A black male reporter would leave, and then I would show up. I could see on the faces of many of my colleagues, white male colleagues especially, the suspicion that I was the "affirmative action" hire. Maybe in the minds of management, that is what I was. I have worked in many newsrooms where reporters were recruited and hand-picked to be groomed for a big anchor job. That never happened for me.

In fact, about halfway through my tour of states and stations, I stuck my neck out and for the first time expressed interest in anchoring a broadcast. It had disastrous consequences. For reasons that will become apparent, I won't mention which city it was. I was actually up for a weekend anchor job since I had been filling in for weeks, but the station was delaying making a decision. The ratings were good and my work was fine, but the company would not pull the trigger. Finally, I pressed my news director, who was a friend. "What's the deal?" I insisted. His response shocked me. His boss, a station executive, had said, "A nigger would never anchor one of my broadcasts." My news director passed on the quotation reluctantly.

"You can sue if you'd like. Then you'll be blackballed and never work in TV. If subpoenaed by a judge, I'd testify to what was said. You can be angry and let it eat you up inside. Or you can press on," he said, with a mix of sadness and disgust in his voice.

It is the one and only time I have ever cried about a job. Not to his face, but when I left the newsroom. I had been polite and shook hands with my boss, and we agreed to re-visit the subject in a few days. This was the first time I was hit squarely in the nose with racism at work. The first thing I did was call my mother. She yelled and fussed with me, and then we prayed. Next, I called my sister. She yelled and fussed with me, and then we prayed. Next, I called my brother. He yelled and fussed with me, then offered to fly into town and meet the offending TV executive in the park-ing lot, and then we prayed. (Funny yet reassuring thing about my family, regardless of the crisis, big or small, the response is always the same. Since I was eight years old, my older brother has always volunteered to fight my battles.)

The next morning my mother called me up early. "What have you decided to do?" she asked. Before I could offer an answer, she gave her opinion. "I think you should just get past it. You didn't go to that job to stay forever. It's just a stop on the journey. Hold your head up. Push your shoulders back. Learn what you're there to learn, and move on," she pleaded.

I knew she was not advocating that I back down. Lord knows Clarice Pitts never shied away from a fight. But, for her, the point wasn't about a man's judgment of me; it was about what God had planned. Later that day, I went to my news director, thanked him for his honesty, and asked for his support when the chance came to move along. He agreed. A few months later I moved on.

Perhaps I should rephrase that. I didn't move on. God moved me along. In fact, most of the jobs I have ever had in television I never applied for. They usually just came along. Trust me, it is not because anyone was beating the bushes looking for me. As best I can tell, I have never been the first choice for any job, rather the second or third choice, but I always tried to reward those who hired me with my best effort, and I thank God for the many second chances He has given me. Like most people, I have sometimes failed to live up to my own expectations. At other times, I have had to work beyond the low expectations of others.

Pretty far along in my career, I was having a pleasant get-to-know-you conversation with an executive at a new station where I had been hired. I had been in the news business for quite a while, had won a few awards, and covered a few major events. It was a discussion about the expectations of the job and where I wanted to take my career. By this time, I was focused on the goal of being a *60 Minutes* correspondent someday. For me, it was the promised land of journalism. I could do everything I wanted to do as a reporter, from investigative work to profiles of the famous and the infamous, and it would be a chance to showcase my writing and my interviewing skills. I expressed that wish quite forcefully. The executive's response surprised me. "Byron, the thing I like most about you is that you are so articulate," she said.

The bubble over my head asked, *"Articulate? Did she just say articulate? That's it? That's what you like most about me? Years of television reporting. And it's not my body of work, my investigative pieces, my writing, or my reporting? You like that I can speak clearly and string a few coherent sentences together?"*

For me, and for many people who look like me, the word

articulate is code for "We presume most black people can't speak, but you can." I have always considered that one of the greatest insults, because it assumes that we would not be able to speak to be understood. I have heard people describe a Colin Powell or a Clarence Thomas as articulate. As if it's a surprise that a secretary of state or a Supreme Court justice could express themselves. And they are the exception to the rule. I never heard anyone describe as articulate Ronald Reagan or Bill Clinton or a single one of my white colleagues. It's as if the greatest attribute for a person of color is that he can speak the English language.

Did this executive declare this because of some deep-rooted racism? Almost certainly not. Maybe she could not think of anything else to say. Or maybe her expectations for me were just that low. That the best I had to offer was that I could speak English. Granted, given my problems with stuttering, at one stage in my life if a person in a position of authority had labeled me articulate, that would have been a reason to shake their hand and shout Hallelujah. But she did not know about my history. That was not her point of reference. For a seasoned broadcast journalist, such a comment was ridiculous.

But in her office I smiled and nodded and thought to myself: She will set limits that I must overcome. Her expectations of me are so limited that she is just one more obstacle I need to remove from my path. From that day forward, I always outwardly respected her opinion but gave it no value.

At age thirty-eight, I finally knew that I was ready. I was hired to be a correspondent by *CBS News* to report the national news. I arrived at CBS with a mixture of gratitude and impatience. From day one on the job, I was already three years behind my own career schedule. But I quickly learned that just getting to the network was not enough to guarantee a successful career. Even though a correspondent has been hired, it is still at the discretion of each individual broadcast executive producer to decide if he or she wants to use that correspondent regularly on the broadcast. Executives have their favorites, who might appear five days a week, and then there are some correspondents who appear rarely. The criteria can be very subjective, ranging from writing skill to voice delivery. After being hired, one can experience a continual process of auditioning for work. It reminded me of Dr. Lewes's lesson in college about learning the style of each professor and then working to please them. I needed to learn what each executive producer wanted if I was going to become a regular part of their broadcast.

Part of that process included establishing personal relationships with the executives. After a correspondent is hired, protocol requires that he or she pay a visit to New York for a sit-down meeting with each executive producer to discuss expectations and any special needs of their broadcasts, from the *CBS Evening News* with Dan Rather to *Sunday Morning* to the (then) *CBS Morning News* (now called *The Early Show*). Essentially, you are shopping your skills.

When I was first hired in 1998, I was in the process of relocating to work in the network's Miami bureau. I was brought to New York for meetings with all the executives, and that visit led me to the office of a particular executive producer at *CBS News* whom I had never met. He had been running the morning program for a number of years. Apparently he was not impressed with what he had seen from me so far. On the day of the appointment, I had shown up at his office a few minutes early. His secretary told me to be seated. We could both hear him on the phone. He took at least three phone calls before finally calling me in to his office about thirty minutes after I had arrived.

"Please take a seat," he said, with his feet hanging over the corner of his desk. "Just give me another moment," he said as he made another phone call.

After a few minutes of cackling on the phone, he turned to me and said, "I don't have much time, so let's get right to it. I don't think you're very good. You don't write well enough to be on my show, and I want only the best correspondents on my show, and that is *not* you," he said, as he spent most of the time searching for something on his desk. He never made eye contact. He went on for a bit longer. When he finally looked up at me and said, "I hope this doesn't hurt your feelings. I'm just giving it to you straight. Nothing personal," he said with a smile. "If there's nothing else, I have some work to do," he said and stood up, gesturing me toward the door.

Like a kid educated in Catholic school, I jumped to my feet and said, "Thank you, sir. I appreciate your honesty and your time." On the inside I wanted to punch him in the nose. Then just before I turned for the door, I stopped, looked back at him, and said something I had never said to any human being before. "I respect what you've said and I respect your position, but please know this: When I'm on my knees praying in my room at night, not once have I ever called your name. My destiny is not in your hands, not now, not ever. Thank you for your time. I'll see you down the road."

He cocked his head to one side and gave me a curious look. I walked out of his office and never appeared on *his* broadcast again. Perhaps he had won the day, but I was not defeated. Funny thing about God, He apparently has a great sense of humor. Less than one year later, the executive was no longer at the helm of the morning program. There's an old Chinese proverb that I have always remembered. "If you stand by the river long enough, you will see the bodies of your enemies float by." It was my intention to stand at the shoreline of CBS for many years to come.

What I have lacked in talent, God has always made up for with His grace. He has fought my battles, protected me in good times and bad. He has given me an optimistic spirit. Optimism is a great gift. It can sustain you when everything around you is falling apart, and when you cannot read, when you are deemed a failure, or when you are considered second best. I have leaned on that optimism more than might have seemed reasonable, and it has always helped me. I needed every bit of my optimism on September 11, 2001.

"Get down to the World Trade Center. There's been an accident," yelled Marty Gill. I had just moved to New York from the South and had never been to the World Trade Center. I had no idea where it was. But since Marty was not normally a yeller, I knew right away something serious had happened. Martin Gill worked the assignment desk for *CBS News*. For years he had been responsible for handing out assignments in the Southern region. When I was based in Miami and later Atlanta for CBS, Marty's was often the voice on the other end of the phone sending me to hurricanes, tornadoes, or any other kind of spot news event. Probably just a few years older than me, he carried himself like a wise old man. Marty knew everything there was to know about satellite trucks and satellite truck drivers, feed points, which local stations had the best photographers, and where his people could get a steak in almost every city and small town in the South, Midwest, and along the eastern seaboard. Born and raised in Michigan, Marty brought Midwestern values and sensibilities to the New York office. He was not flashy or loud. He was just solid.

That morning I could hear the excitement in Marty's voice and see it in his eyes when he leaned into my office. "I need you down at the World Trade Center now, brother," he said with an increasing sense of urgency. I had not moved the first time he called me.

I had come to work early, before the crowds, intent on finishing up the script for another project. It was a profile of actor Harry Belafonte for the CBS broadcast *Sunday Morning*. I was not really up for chasing a spot news story.

"What happened?" I asked, with sarcasm hanging from every word.

"A plane hit the World Trade Center. You need to go," Marty said as he stormed out of my office and back to the national desk. With that, I grabbed my work bag and suit coat and walked outside.

"Can you get me to the World Trade Center?" I asked the yellow cab driver. Without turning around (New York cab drivers never do), he said, "Yeah! Did you hear what happened? A plane just hit one of the Twin Towers."

At this point, I was thinking that a novice pilot in a small plane must have gone off course and hit the building. But the closer we got, the more obvious it became that I was wrong. This was big. Fire trucks and ambulances rushed past the cab, and in the distance flames and billowing smoke were visible from both towers.

We were both stunned at what we were seeing. "I can't get you any closer. You gotta walk from here," the cabbie said when we got about twenty blocks from the epicenter of the disaster. He never asked for the fare. I never offered to pay. I just got out of the cab and started walking. People were in the street, running away from the buildings. Police officers had already set up barricades and were directing emergency vehicles in. It was loud and chaotic. There wasn't as much a sense of fear in the air as there was confusion. Word was spreading that it was two commercial planes that hit the buildings. Reality was sinking in. This was not an accident. This was terrorism. Any question of who did it and the why seemed irrelevant at the time. I finally was close enough to the buildings to talk with a group of police officers. One plainclothesman, the others in uniform. They were looking straight up.

"What is that?" one of them yelled as he pointed. We all looked. It resembled a large sheet of paper floating to the ground. I thought maybe it was someone from one of the upper floors sending a message, à la the Columbine High School massacre. Perhaps it was someone pleading for help. As this object dropped faster and closer to us, we realized it wasn't paper. It was a woman wearing a dress. She was falling. There were at least a handful of people falling. The officers and I watched in stunned silence.

"Look up there," another one of the officers yelled. High above, we saw what looked like two people standing on a window ledge. They took hands and jumped. They held on to each other for a short distance and then let go. We followed their fall. It was more horrifying than the first. One of the officers vomited. We all turned away.

As I was trying to keep it together, and beginning to think about what part of the story I would work on, I spotted my colleague *CBS News* correspondent Mika Brzezinski. By this time every reporter in New York was dispatched to lower Manhattan. Not long after Mika and I exchanged hellos, the story was about to change.

"It's coming down," someone yelled. Chunks of the World Trade Center's south tower were falling to the ground. In that moment, any sense of confusion turned to sheer panic. Every person was running, and that included Mika and me. Mika quickly kicked off her shoes and grabbed them; I grasped her hand and we ran as fast as we could. We made it to an elementary school that was being evacuated. The students were all but gone. We crowded inside with police, firefighters, and every other straggler who sprinted in. Chased up the street by thick black smoke, we all waited inside in dead silence. There was a rumbling that sounded like an earthquake. As suddenly as it started, it stopped. One of the firefighters walked out first, and then a few more were joined by police officers. Mika and I had found a phone in the school and managed to contact the national desk. All the networks were live on the air. Mika and I agreed that she would give the first account by phone while I walked outside to get more information. The air was so thick with dust and debris that it was difficult to breathe. I have long carried a handkerchief in my pocket for no good reason. I finally had a good reason. It felt like I was wandering around the surface of the moon. Everything was covered in white. A powdery soft dust covered the ground, cars, buildings, and most of the people.

I would later describe the day on the air this way: "Except for a few sirens, I have never heard New York City this quiet. Graveyard quiet." That is what it felt like those early moments after the first tower fell. It felt like I was standing in a graveyard or on the moon. Minutes later, the second tower collapsed, and once again everyone who could ran for cover. During the next hours I would see acts of bravery and kindness we do not spend enough time talking about in our country. Most people were so dusty it was hard to tell a person's race or even sometimes their sex. People of all description were helping the injured reach safety. I watched business people in suits and dresses tearing at their clothing to make a bandage or a brace. I watched one man kneel and pray in the middle of the street.

We interviewed a firefighter covered in dust from head to toe. He had brown eyes. I could see only a streak of his skin, revealed as tears rolled down from his eyes. "I lost my men," he told me. How many, I asked. "All of them," he said. With that, he turned away and walked back toward the pile. Within a few days, ordinary New Yorkers had formed a gauntlet down the West Side highway. At night they would applaud the emergency teams and construction workers as they changed shifts. People brought their children, and they carried food and water. This was rough, tough New York City, and for those first few days after the towers fell, I never heard a single word of profanity. There was a sense of peace and purpose and strength at Ground

Zero that is hard to fathom except for those of us who were there.

The world was upside down. I had witnessed the end of a life more than a few times in my career—a man put to death in Virginia's electric chair, a stabbing victim who bled to death in an Atlanta hospital. None of that prepared me for what I was seeing. But there wasn't much time to dwell on it or mourn. On September 11, 2001, and on many days like it, I found it best to hide behind my job. Reporters are supposed to keep some detachment from the people and the subjects in their reporting. It was that professional distance that kept me grounded in the notion that I was placed in this moment to cover history not get caught up in it. It was not about me or particularly what I was feeling, it was about the people around me and reporting on their experiences, their emotions, and not my own.

History will recall the horrors of that time, and there were many. As an optimist, I choose to also remember the good and decent people of that day.

TEN

Valley of the Shadow of Death

Yea, though I walk through the valley of the shadow of death, I will fear no evil: for thou *art* with me. . . .

—Psalm 23:4

Do you know all the people you love most in the world?"

"Yes, sir, I do," I answered with a kind of awkward do-I-or-don't-I-smile expression one often wears in the boss's office. The boss in this case was *CBS News* anchorman Dan Rather. We were sitting in his office on the second floor above the newsroom, Dan in his leather chair and me in a straightbacked, stiff, wooden chair in front of his massive desk, discussing my upcoming trip to cover the post-9/11 war in Afghanistan. It was fairly standard practice that a difficult overseas assignment would merit a warmup pep talk from Dan.

"Okay, then write each of them a letter, tell them exactly how important they are to you. Address the letters, seal them up, and leave them in your desk drawer so someone will find them in case you don't come home," he said. Then he just let the words hang in the air for a while. If he was trying to get a reaction out of me, he didn't. I kept my expression calm. Inside, I was wondering how this conversation was supposed to help me. I was hoping to be encouraged, not frightened.

Since there was no natural light in the office, the cavelike darkness often made it difficult to make out all of Dan's features. In dramatic fashion, it was slightly reminiscent of a scene from *The Godfather*, dim light, dark wood, an imposing figure behind the desk, and a much-worn trench coat hanging on the door. Instead of a gun or cigar box, however, he kept a Bible on his desk, which left a comparable impression.

"When you go to a place like Afghanistan," he continued, "you might not come back. That may sound harsh, but it's true. If you can't handle that truth, then you shouldn't go. If you can, go with God's speed. And remember three more things about Afghanistan. Don't eat the meat, don't drink the water, and never look at the women," Rather said, with a smile growing on the edges of his lips.

"I'm glad you're going," Rather said. "Birds gotta fly, fish gotta swim, and reporters gotta go."

"Reporters gotta go." I certainly lived by that creed. By 2001 I had established myself as a network fireman, volunteering for every major story, both domestic and foreign. I had worked in both the Miami and Atlanta bureaus covering the 2000 election recount in Florida, the tug of war over Cuba's Elian Gonzalez, and numerous natural disasters. I had traveled abroad to Iraq, Central and South America, and Haiti. But less than two months after September 11, when the network was seeking volunteers for coverage in

Afghanistan, I had hesitated. For the first time in my professional life, I had to ask myself whether the job was simply too dangerous for me, whether I really needed to be in a place actively involved in bloodletting, like Afghanistan in 2001. Without trying to sound morbid, there are reasons to die, causes worth dying for, like family or one's faith. But did my career ambition require that I take this risk with my life?

I was afraid. Have you ever been afraid? So afraid you couldn't move? Have you ever been shaken by the kind of fear that makes your eyes water and your nose run? When I was a child, fear would usually take me by the hand and lead me away from danger and difficult situations. Fear, just like anger, was a friend of mine. Now in my early forties I had done a pretty good job of keeping my fears at a distance. Journalists at this stage don't talk much about being afraid. One of the things that drew me to this profession in the first place was the bravery associated with it. I remembered seeing and reading about reporters who endured threats during the civil rights protest era or those who went on countless patrols alongside soldiers in Vietnam. Those were the risky datelines of their generation, and America was better because of their courage. Now history was calling on my generation. Being a journalist in wartime does not compare to the hardships and risks facing America's sons and daughters in the U.S. military or the demands heaped upon their families. Theirs is a special calling, but reporting from dangerous places carries its own risks, and a number of journalists around the world have given their full measure in search of truth. So after some soul searching, prayer, and a few intense conversations with family, I put my name on the list of those who would go to Afghanistan.

And after Dan's "pep talk," I wrote the letters to my loved ones as he recommended. (They are still in my office desk, and I pray I get to turn those letters into paper planes with my grandchildren someday.) Normally I was excited to go away on big assignments, looked forward to packing my bags, and enjoyed the process of counting out batteries and socks and maps. This time I felt more like I was packing to go to a funeral. I wasn't excited. I was too nervous to be excited. In the past, my foreign assignments would have been dangerous only by accident. In covering the war in Afghanistan, death wasn't an accident; it was a consequence. But before my fears got the best of me, I did what I was raised to do: I prayed.

Days later, I left for Russia and traveled from there to the capital of Tajikistan for the long car ride to the Afghanistan border. I met up with a few journalists from other news organizations, and we took a short ride on a raft across the Amu Darya River. It felt a bit like traveling backward in a time machine: thirty-six hours earlier I had been in a fine Russian hotel near Red Square and then aboard a jetliner from Moscow. Suddenly I was floating across a fairly deep river, with strangers, on a motorized raft. No one said a word, which is unusual for a group of journalists. Usually there is at least one person in these groups who wants to share how much they know about the place we're going to. But except for the two Russian guides who spoke no English, no one on the raft had ever been to Afghanistan before. It's one thing to be scared. It's another to see it in the eyes of everyone around you. I had been to the developing world before, but as we floated to the shoreline, Afghanistan looked like a place struggling to reach developing-world status. I could see mud huts and decades-old vehicles. A stench of burning charcoal was in the air, and men huddled around small campfires were cooking what appeared to be goat.

My only instructions were that an Afghani would meet me on the shore to take me to the CBS compound. I walked up the riverbank carrying my own gear and dragging two cases of equipment for the crews. At this point I was more of a packmule than a journalist, bringing in fresh supplies. I guess I was expecting the kind of welcome greeting I would have gotten at an airport, a nice man holding a sign with my name on it. What I got was a thickly built bearded Afghan man with a Kalashnikov rifle on his shoulder, carrying a CBS mailbag. He looked like he was in a bad mood. I put my right hand to my heart and said, "Hello, sir, I'm Byron Pitts." His expression didn't change. He didn't move, just looked right through me. I stepped forward and extended my hand and repeated, "Hello, sir, I'm Byron Pitts from *CBS News*." That got his attention. He took two steps forward and pushed my chest with both hands. I hadn't come across that greeting in all the books I had read about Afghanistan. More than surprised, I was puzzled as to why this man was touching me. About that time, he took another step and pushed me again. I looked around and saw other Afghan men standing and looking at us. The other journalists had filtered away. Then I looked down and realized that I was standing on the edge of the riverbank. If he pushed me again, I would fall into the water. When he reached up to push me one more time, I grabbed his hands and pushed him back hard. I was half expecting him to raise his weapons. Instead, he smiled. I guess I passed the test. He turned and gestured toward his ancient Russian pickup truck. As I got into his truck, I thought about how unfamiliar this environment was, how aggressive this culture was, and how careful I would need to be.

CBS News had a base camp in northern Afghanistan, in an empty stretch of windswept land masquerading as a village called Khoja Bahauddin (we pronounced it *Hoja-Baha-Who-Dean*). The region looked like one of those planets from an early episode of *Lost in Space* or the way the Old West might have looked long before it was settled. Living was hard: the place was dry and dusty, with most of its people living at different rungs of desperation. On windy days some of us would joke about the time and money Westerners spent on exfoliates and such to clear up their skin. Spend a brief time in Khoja Bahauddin, and the mixture of desert sand and Mother Nature would buff your skin to a baby-soft shine. Spend too much time, and you could age dramatically. We would meet men in their thirties, windblown and sunburned, who looked to be in their seventies. We were indeed foreigners in a foreign land. Language seemed the least of our barriers.

Before 9/11, most Americans knew little and perhaps cared even less about Afghanistan. The United States had shown passing interest in the region during the 1980s when the country was at war with the Soviet Union. September 11 changed all that. Osama bin Laden had claimed responsibility for the terror attack on the United States, and his organi-

zation, Al Qaeda, had ties to Afghanistan and its ruling
Taliban party. While the Taliban ruled, a tribal militia group
called the Northern Alliance had been battling for control,
region by region, for years. Their commander, Ahmad Shah
Massoud, was assassinated two days before the terror attack
in New York. Now the Northern Alliance had a friend in the
United States.

We were assigned to the northern region of Afghanistan.
Our job was to file news reports on the efforts by the Northern Alliance to push their way south to the capital city of
Kabul, while they engaged in all-out combat or minor skir-
mishes with the Taliban fighters. We would get daily brief-
ings from our colleagues at the Pentagon about the major
movements of the battle, but we mostly relied on our local
interpreters to tell us how close we could get to the front day
to day. We filed regularly for the *CBS Evening News* and *The
Early Show* the next morning. One day we reported on the
fierce battle for a village. Another day it was the reopening
of a village bazaar, where people could shop for goods and
men could shave their beards. Other network teams were
coming into Afghanistan from the east and the south. We
were all hoping to meet in Kabul, where many of us naively
thought the war might end.

To travel abroad for a major news organization is something akin to being a part of a traveling circus, a rock band,
or a very large family. Engineers, technicians, photographers,
producers, and editors—these are the people television viewers never see and rarely hear about—are all separated from
their loved ones for long stretches of time, often longer stints
than the on-air reporters. Their days can stretch from dawn

until bedtime—preparing for daily assignments, coordinating the teams, and keeping in communication with headquarters. Back home, assignment-desk and logistics folks make it all work. Add to it the bad food, poor sleeping arrangements, bouts of dysentery, plus the occasional burst of gunfire and explosives. No one was under any illusion that this was a vacation in paradise.

On big overseas stories, technicians traveled from around the world, so we were sometimes meeting for the very first time. Francesca Neidbart, a sound technician from Austria, was partnered in Afghanistan with her cameraman husband, Alex Brucker. I had never met Francesca until I actually bumped into her one night inside the compound near the kitchen. She's a beautiful woman, with olive skin and thick black hair; I thought she was an Afghan woman roaming around after dark and remembered Dan's warning, "Never look at the women." Here was a woman with her hair uncovered. I panicked, bowed my head, and backed out of the room like an uncoordinated attempt at the moonwalk. I knocked over a case of water, which knocked over a stack of pots and pans. The loud chain reaction woke up the entire compound. On top of all the built-in stresses, we were living on top of one another and couldn't escape for a moment's peace.

Leading the CBS operation was a legendary producer named Larry Doyle. If John Wayne had ever worked as a network producer, he would have trained under Larry Doyle. The kind of rugged toughness that Wayne symbolized in Hollywood, Larry, a captain in the U.S. Marine Corps during Vietnam, commanded in the field of journalism. He had nearly translucent, penetrating blue eyes, a voice like Humphrey Bogart, matched with thick, wavy black and silvery hair, and a solid frame. Larry was a mess of contradictions. If you saw Larry at work, he was almost always disheveled, like a guy who didn't care about his appearance. He had a perpetual three o'clock shadow closing in on four o'clock, usually a cigarette and a Heineken in hand, deck shoes, and an untucked open shirt. But if you met Larry at a social event outside work, at a colleague's party or at dinner, he would be dressed to the nines. In such settings he was a guy who seemed very fashion-conscious, with a wardrobe of delicate fabrics, like silks and linens. It was clear that besides the valuable experiences he had picked up in various war zones, he had also done quite a bit of shopping. He staffed the Afghanistan office, as he had other locations, with beer, cigarettes, candy bars, beef jerky, and the best local drivers and interpreters around.

During one innocent moment when I first met him, I asked Larry, "Do we have anything besides beer? I don't drink beer." He never answered, just stared a hole in my head with his bright blue eyes rimmed with heavy bags from a lifetime of little sleep. I finally got the message, opened a beer, and shut up. Less because of the age difference and more because of his demeanor, Larry was like everyone's favorite uncle on the road, a bit dangerous, worldly, protective, and wise. As a relatively young correspondent, I worked with Larry in Afghanistan, Iraq, Central America, and throughout the United States. He was at times a friend, a parent, a coach, a confidant, and on occasion a pain in the butt. Each and every time he was what I needed. He was a truth teller on those days when the truth was not particularly pleasant to hear. He taught me to never go into a story with preconceived notions; always have a plan of escape and a backup plan. He taught me the meaning of professional loyalty. If it is a bar, a knife fight, or a trip to Afghanistan, you want Larry Doyle on your side. For all the weeks we were in Afghanistan, he made my top-ten prayer list each and every night. "Lord, thank you for Larry."

The CBS compound was guarded twenty-four hours a day by a dozen armed Afghanis. In the middle of this desolate, poverty-stricken region was about an acre of expensive, high-tech equipment worth hundreds of thousands of dollars, plus a significant amount of cash. We were a potential target. But the guards never traveled with us on any of our assignments. After several days in the country, the storyline and the war forced us to head south toward central Afghanistan. That meant leaving the comfort and security of our compound behind. I left with Larry, cameraman Mark Laganga, and CBS radio reporter Phil Ittner, along with three drivers and an interpreter. For our team, getting to Kabul meant traveling over two hundred miles of open desert, through small villages and scattered towns, with more than a few pitched battles between the Northern Alliance and the Taliban along the way. The challenge was to stay close enough to track the ongoing battle but far enough away to keep safe. We often talked about the pros and cons of carrying a weapon for our own protection, but we were observers of this conflict, not participants. Having a gun might have emboldened us to take an unnecessary risk. We always felt safer with some proximity to the troops, because without weapons or the protection of military forces, as journalists we were fully exposed to the violence of the region. There was also the fact that we were known to carry supplies and money. Bandits were about as common as rocks. Every day we made a threat assessment before we ventured out to shoot our story. How close could we get to the violence without getting caught in the crossfire? How dangerous were the roads?

One day we woke up early, packed, and were headed down a road that we knew to be a shortcut to the next village. Suddenly a local farmer shouted to one of our interpreters, telling us to stop. The road had been filled with landmines by the Taliban. We couldn't see the mines, but we trusted his word and turned our vehicles around. It was difficult to comprehend that we were just a shout away from almost certain catastrophe. We were relieved to be alive but angry that our own interpreter had not known the terrain well enough to protect us. We were paying him not just to speak the language but to guide us where we needed to go.

About two days out from Khoja Bahauddin, we were standing on the wrong side of the Kokcha River and needed to cross. The only way seemed to be by horseback. We had too much gear and too few vehicles to handle the weight. We were at risk of sinking into the muddy bottom. To make matters worse, it was growing dark. We had to reach the nearest village, on the other side of the river, before nightfall. It never failed to happen that the darker it became outside, the shadier the characters would become around us. Our interpreter told Larry the mood along the riverbank was changing. Some of the new arrivals at the river were debating whether to rob us.

That's when we heard a voice in the distance. "Larry! Larry Doyle, is that you, mate?" The voice came from an Australian journalist named Paul McGeough, who was sitting alongside the riverbank. He recognized Larry from a previous encounter, on a trip to Iraq. McGeough quickly assessed our problem and called in some support vehicles to help us across a shallow stretch of water. We soon learned that Paul had just endured what we all feared as journalists, an attack that left three of his colleagues dead. The night before, Paul had been with a group of journalists traveling with a Northern Alliance commander. The group was ambushed by Taliban fighters. Of the six journalists, three were killed and three survived. Paul was one of the survivors. He was headed out, not for home, mind you, but just for some other part of Afghanistan.

"Never leave a story on a bad note," McGeough said. Paul and Larry greeted each other with great affection, like long-lost brothers. Clearly, Paul needed the emotional support after his ordeal. After introductions were made, we quickly decided that Paul's story should be part of our report for the next night's *CBS Evening News*. We interviewed him right where we found him, by the side of the river.

(The *CBS Evening News*, November 12, 2001)
Today, United Front Soldiers counted their bounty after the bloodiest weekend in this war so far. In what seemed like 72 straight hours of rocket launches, attacks,

and counterattacks, much was gained here and much was lost.

These were the rocket launchers and rifles, boots and sleeping bags, taken off the bodies of Taliban soldiers killed in battle.

[Byron speaks with commander]
"Your tanks killed 27 Taliban soldiers."

This tank commander boasted of running over 27 wounded Taliban soldiers. "It was easier," he said, "than taking prisoners."

There were prisoners and prized trophies. This letter was taken from a dead Taliban soldier written on the stationery of "The Islamic Front," one of bin Laden's terrorist cells in Pakistan.

[Byron, with interpreter]
"I know they are bombing on you. So be strong. I know God will protect you."

For the first time, civilians in Northern Afghanistan were allowed back into villages once controlled by the Taliban. Cross the Kokcha River, they were told. It's SAFE to go home.

[Byron on camera]
But safety is a slippery word in war. Sunday night six journalists accompanied a United Front commander to survey a town that had just been declared safe. Three of

the six journalists were gunned down. Shot to death as they scrambled for cover.

[Byron interview with Paul McGeough of the *Sydney Morning Herald*]
"Suddenly we were being fired upon from three sides."

Paul McGeough is one of three journalists who survived.

[More interview with McGeough]
"We were ambushed. And probably the nastiest thing of all, the bodies were looted by the time we got to them this morning."

McGeough admits he GAINED a story but LOST three friends.

[More interview with McGeough]
"But if you combine the losses on both sides on that ridge last night, apart from the media, there were 110 people killed."

What do you take from what you lived through?

"Thank God I'm alive. It was very scary and it doesn't make me want to pack up and go home. But it makes me, it makes me . . . I want to be close to someone."

Gains and losses. On one weekend in one nation at war. Byron Pitts, CBS News.

That night over hot tea and two fried potatoes cooked with oil on our hot plate, the five of us ate. Larry had convinced Paul to join us. We were glad to have his company and his knowledge of the region. Now, five of us were slowly moving south toward Kabul. Every day was physically draining. We would work eighteen to twenty hours a day, with very little sleep. We used bottled water and wet wipes for hygiene. There was not much food. Some days we would climb for hours on the dusty hills to get a better view of the battle. Our vehicles were often breaking down. Three of us would have to hold up the truck while a tire was being changed. One night we'd sleep in an abandoned building, another night on the rocky ground under the stars. Then there was the constant stress of wondering if the Taliban would overtake us or if bandits might find us. On a night when we finally found shelter from the cold in an abandoned schoolhouse, we were in desperate need of a good night's sleep. It didn't take any time for all of us to fall into a sound sleep. But when we were startled awake by a scratching sound, our first panicked thought was that it was an intruder. Mark Laganga saw it first—a large rat. Mark sarcastically suggested we catch it and eat it. Phil and I were in the room with it and wanted no part of the hairy creature. Larry ended the discussion.

"That rat lives here! We're the intruders. Quit your griping and get some sleep!" Later that night, he whispered to me, "If you want to switch places with me, you can." We all got a big laugh out of it, which we needed as much as sleep. It made us feel normal and gave us something else to talk about for a few hours at least.

Eventually, Paul would leave us, after he filed his share of stories and could end his trip on a good note. We parted ways as Paul waited in an open field to catch a ride from a Russian-made helicopter, north toward the Tajikistan border. As we pulled away, Paul waved good-bye. A single black bag hung from his shoulder. All he needed he could carry on his back, like a seasoned war correspondent.

A few weeks into the Afghanistan trip, I came down with a wicked bout of dysentery. I could not keep anything down and spent most of the day on my back or in the makeshift bathroom Laganga had rigged up. We affectionately referred to him as McGyver. (For the uninitiated, that's the name of a nineties' TV show about a guy who could get himself out of the most dangerous situations with as little as a toothpick and a piece of string.) Laganga could fix anything. There were not many restrooms in northern Afghanistan at the time. Mark took four pieces of tin, a milk crate, a shovel, a coat hanger, and a roll of toilet paper, and built a toilet— with running water, sort of. Although there was not enough tin for an actual door, Mark came up with the idea of a red bandana. If the red bandana was hanging on a hook in front of the bathroom, that meant no one should walk in front of it lest they and the person inside be surprised. When I was sick, that bandana was always in use. After about four days on my back on a cot, Larry tracked down a local doctor who spoke English. Actually, he was a veterinarian, but desperate times called for creative measures.

"Mr. Byron, what seems to be the problem?" the doctor asked, with a gentle bedside manner that surpassed plenty of American doctors I had encountered. I explained my symptoms. "What medicine do you take, Mr. Byron?" he inquired. Each of us had been issued a supply of Ciprofloxacin in the event of a bacterial infection. The bottle said take two tablets per day. I remember the doctor back in the States insisting I take no more than the prescribed amount each day because of side effects.

The Afghan animal doctor asked how many pills I took per day, and when I said two, he asked with a puzzled look on his face, "Why just two, Mr. Byron?" When I explained the concerns raised by the American doctor, he burst out laughing.

"Oh no, Mr. Byron, this is Afghanistan! Don't worry about side effects. Please take eight pills tomorrow." With that, he shook my hand. "You will feel better in a few days, Mr. Byron, I promise. Inshallah [God willing]," he said, as he left my side. Sure enough, two days later I was up and running, as if I had never been sick. In good shape for the head-on collision that was about to occur.

Like many things in Afghanistan, driving seemed like another test of manhood and another needless escalation of tension. In a convoy of vehicles, drivers would take turns jockeying to be in the lead. On narrow dusty roads, drivers were often blinded by the dust created by the car in front of them. Larry had arranged for a convoy of Toyota-style pickup trucks to take us south. I ended up in a burgundy vehicle, in the hands of a teenage driver with a collection of bad local music. Funny thing about teenage drivers around the world; they are all about the same, hard of hearing and fearless.

Our vehicle was about fourth in line when my young

driver decided it was his turn to lead the pack. So he dashed out into oncoming traffic to make his way to the front. Most drivers coming toward us just moved aside and honked their horns. However, the driver of an approaching large truck with people piled on top did not appear willing to concede the road. In my calmest East Baltimore tone, I whispered to the driver, "Hey, brother, do you see that big truck?" I quickly assessed that the young man spoke no English, and I took a different approach with more attitude and bass in my voice. "Yo, man! Do you see that big-ass truck?" He looked at me and smiled. He didn't understand a word I said, but he seemed to enjoy the panic in my voice and on my face. He turned his attention away from me toward the road and waved his hand at the truck, like a guy waving a fly off the windshield of his car. The truck driver apparently did not take kindly to the gesture. Just as we were about to hit the truck head-on, both drivers gave just a little bit but a little too late. We collided. Not a full-on front-end collision, but the front-right corner of our truck hit the front of their vehicle, which was about twice our size. Our pickup did a 180-degree spin and was thrown into a ditch, facing the direction we had come from. The bigger truck came to a stop on the opposite side of the highway. A passenger hanging off the top of the truck was thrown into the desert.

Dazed and grateful, I was still conscious, with a fast-moving headache that started at the back of my neck. I waited for the dust and sand to clear. Thank God we were both wearing our seat belts. As I lay there, the driver began yelling and pulling at my seat belt. Did he think I was injured? Perhaps he was trying to help me? Then I realized he was not clawing at my seat belt. He was trying to climb over me. His door was jammed. To hell with the American, he was trying to get away. About that time I noticed the driver from the truck and a few other men running toward our vehicle with pipes in their hands. They were yelling. I couldn't make out the language, of course, but their volume suggested they urgently wanted a conversation with my driver. By the time the men got to our vehicle, the driver was out the door and running down the road. All I could see was the bottom of his shoes and a small cloud of dust. Larry and Mark ran to see if I was okay. I was shaken a bit but otherwise fine. We repacked my gear into one of the other vehicles. When we inquired about the driver and his car, one of our interpreters said, "Do not worry. Local justice." With that, we moved on.

The pace of our travel was determined by the progression of the Northern Alliance push to the south. Some days they would gain several square miles and any handful of villages. The next day they might lose a third of it, as the Taliban would push back. That give-and-take of war dictated our timetable and our travel schedule. We knew that a major battle would eventually take place in the large city of Konduz, currently a Taliban stronghold. The Northern Alliance had to take control of it to secure a major supply route to the south. We traveled through a series of nameless villages on our way to Konduz. Tribal clans ran each town, and we needed to get permission for safe travel or an overnight stay.

After a week of sleeping under the stars fewer than fifty miles from Konduz, we found comfortable indoor accommodations just in time for Thanksgiving. It was a compound that had been abandoned by a local doctor fleeing from the Taliban. Relatively speaking, it was a nice two-story mud structure. There were multiple bedrooms because the doctor had multiple wives. No beds, no furniture, but we each carried our own cots to our own private rooms. Generally, we did not allow ourselves much time to think about our families back home. But it was a holiday, and I think we were all a bit melancholy. Mark was the most recently married. He decided to make Thanksgiving a special meal. Mark spotted a bird, which we believed to be a duck. While we worked, the household cook killed it, plucked it, and grilled it. Add some rice and beans, and we were ready for the feast. We were thrilled, because it was different from the goat, rice, or noodles that we ate most days after we ran out of beef jerky and Vienna sausages. Yet it was like a bad picnic. The duck was dark, stringy, and kind of bloody, not really cooked all the way through. No one complained. It was as close to home as we could get.

It was a nice respite but a brief one. The Northern Alliance was moving, and we had to move with them. Konduz was a few hours away; the battle was now imminent. Leaving after sunrise gave us ample time to make the trip in daylight, if there were no delays, no transportation breakdowns, and nothing unexpected happened. But we had to decide if we were going to push into darkness. Larry, who had been on the most overseas assignments, had a few basic rules that he insisted upon for safety. Never travel alone, never flash money in public, and never travel at night. But if we did not get to the outskirts of Konduz in the next few hours, we ran the risk of missing the action entirely. We took a vote, and there was unanimous agreement to push the limit of daylight and get to the next location in time to make air. Our maps indicated that a fairly routine trip was ahead of us. If everything went right on the road to Konduz, we would make it before nightfall. Unfortunately, very little went right.

Our interpreters provided a handmade map, which indicated a well-traveled road leading to Konduz. What our map failed to show was that the primary route, a narrow gravel road through the region, had recently been destroyed by the Taliban. We had to turn our convoy around and return to the last village to ask for help finding the best way south. The villagers put us on a road that was traveled more by animals than vehicles. The craters and rocks were hell on our trucks' transmissions and tires. Of the five vehicles we started with, three broke down by midday. Two of the drivers refused to leave their broken-down trucks, and another driver abandoned us when he grew frightened by the unfamiliar route. In the next village, we downsized our gear, leaving behind water and some of our camping equipment. We bought another truck for cash and picked up a cocky sixteen-year-old driver who was willing to make the trip. Despite the language barrier, negotiations always came down to the number of one-hundred-dollar bills we were prepared to hand over.

We had lost a few hours, and it was now closing in on the afternoon. Mindful of the time pressure, with our new driver and a not-so-new vehicle, we set off on our way. We were still on a back road without any map to guide us. I was in the front car of the caravan, with the new driver and an English-speaking guide. Laganga was in the middle vehicle, with one of our original drivers and the fixer/cook/handyman. Larry was riding shotgun in the third vehicle, with a driver and our interpreter. The three vehicles stayed in contact by handheld radio. The road was more like a dirt path, carved by nomads, merchants, and drug dealers. Since it was too late to turn back and too dangerous to stop, we kept going amid growing darkness. No one in my vehicle spoke. The only sounds were loud Afghan music and the occasional groan from a pothole. Then without warning the driver slammed on the brakes. He spoke and gestured to the guide, who then turned to me with a pained expression.

"What's wrong?" I asked.

Through broken English, he explained that we had mistakenly driven into an area marked for landmines. During the war in the eighties the Russians had left an estimated seventy thousand landmines in northern Afghanistan. Someone would have to lead us out. I relayed the information by radio to Larry and Mark.

"Any volunteers?" I asked, hoping humor might disguise my fear. My request was met with dead silence. Then Larry spoke up.

"We're paying the guide to guide, so goddamn it, get out of the truck and guide!"

And so he did, on foot. He was a middle-aged man, with a thin frame buried beneath oversized clothes and a face worn by years of conflict. Guided by the headlights of our pickup and the words of the Koran, we crawled along this way with our guide, the human bomb-sniffing interpreter walking in front of three vehicles for about thirty minutes. The cars were barely moving, but we soon reached the end of the minefield. Before we could celebrate safe passage, our teen-ager driver had stopped again. This time he was pointing out of the car and shouting. It turned out we were completely lost and most likely in territory controlled by the Taliban. Not good news. The guide, who had just recovered from his hazardous duty outside the car, now explained that a house off in the distance to our right should be off to our left. In all likelihood we were driving on the wrong side of the nearby mountain. We had little time to figure out how it happened because he could see shadows moving about in the house and was convinced that they were Taliban fighters. I delivered this alarming news to my colleagues in the other two vehicles. As I was explaining our current dilemma, those shadowy figures off to our right (most likely a good half mile away, although it looked closer) jumped in the vehicles outside the house and appeared headed our way.

Larry screamed into the radio, "Go as fast as you can!"

In the desert, "fast as you can" sounded more impressive than it was. We moved at a crawl. The scene would have been comical if it wasn't so frightening. We were in a high-speed chase on an Afghan desert road, but we would have moved faster by foot. The terrain seemed to change with almost every heartbeat. One moment we were in a wide-open area, the next driving down a narrow path with only a few inches on either side of the doors. Not enough space to even open the doors but positioned perfectly to be ambushed. At other turns, we were forced to drive forward a few feet, make a hard turn in the direction we just came from, in order to eventually go forward. It felt as if we were rats in a maze. I have never been more frightened in my life. Then my fear turned to anger. I had promised my wife and children I would do nothing foolish that would risk my life and their future. Eventually, anger turned to sadness. I was about to die. It had happened before in this lawless, forsaken country. Why shouldn't it happen to us? Journalists had no protection here.

Then I began to think about Larry and Mark. What about Larry's wife and children? What had we done? As we bumped along, I actually began to cry. Quietly, with my head down and my fingers in a death grip on the driver's seat in front of me. The paralysis of fear was setting in. I was giving up. I had stopped looking out the window or communicating with Larry and Mark by radio. I should have been helping to navigate our path or offering words of encouragement. I couldn't speak. I couldn't move. Eventually, I closed my eyes and tried to pray. I was so afraid that I could not remember a single Bible verse, even my mother's favorite prayer. So I forced my eyes open to look out my window and see if the end was near.

It was then, for the first time, that I noticed the sky. It was clear. The stars were bright and we were in a valley. It was a breathtaking sight. And then it hit me like a blow to the chest. The Scripture began ringing in my ears. It was Psalm 23:4-6.

Yea, though I walk through the valley of the shadow of death, I will fear no evil: for thou *art* with me; Thy rod and thy staff they comfort me. Thou preparest a table before me in the presence of mine enemies: Thou anointest my head with oil; my cup runneth over. Surely goodness and mercy shall follow me all the days of my life: And I will dwell in the house of the Lord for ever.

In the time it took to say those words, a peace I had never experienced before came over me. In an instant, I felt safer than I had ever felt. I began to realize that nothing Larry or I or Mark or the drivers might do right at that moment would necessarily make a difference. If it was God's will we die, then we would soon be dead. But if it was God's will we live, it would not even matter if the men chasing us caught us. My heart stopped racing. I stopped panting. I wasn't in danger. I was in God's hands, and I knew that was more than enough. What power comes from the sort of peace that no man can give and no man can take away.

The car chase went on for about forty minutes. As it happened, the men in the vehicles behind us never got close and eventually turned away. When we finally made it to the safety of our next desolate accommodation, I did not share my spiritual moment with Larry and Mark. Instead, Larry offered me more earthly solace, a shot of whiskey. Mark gave me one of his cigarettes. I gulped down the whiskey, lit and smoked the cigarette. Looking on in amazement at his colleague who does not drink or smoke, Mark jokingly said, "Byron, at this rate we'll have you snorting cocaine soon." We burst into laughter and then took care of the work that needed to get done. Within a few hours we were all asleep.

We would have other terrifying days and nights in Afghanistan. Not long after the battle of Konduz, a Swedish journalist was awakened by bandits storming a compound packed with journalists in the city of Taloqan. He was shot and killed. Our team was sleeping about one hundred yards away. The screaming of his friends woke us up. We spent the rest of that night comforting one another and talking about how soon we could go home. The next morning nearly everyone in the compound packed their gear and joined a caravan headed north, to leave the country. We had all agreed the story was no longer worth the risk. In all, eight journalists were killed in seventeen days in Afghanistan, including those who had traveled with our friend Paul McGeough. It was a staggering casualty rate for journalists working in a war zone.

When soldiers return home from war, they talk about their comrades, their brothers in arms. Theirs is a bond formed in mud and sweat and sometimes blood. For the rest of my life, I will have that bond with Larry Doyle and Mark Laganga. We don't talk much anymore, but we don't have to.

ELEVEN

Love the Least of Us

For I was an hungred, and ye gave me meat: I was thirsty, and ye gave me drink: I was a stranger, and ye took me in.
—**Matthew 25:35**

WORKING FOR *CBS NEWS* has been a wonderful education. Veterans call it seeing the world on the company's dime. I guess that's true. As much as it's taught me about the places I've been, it's also taught me a few things about myself.

Fear was one of the biggest traits I carried from childhood into adulthood. Selfishness was another. All my life I have been blessed by people who had nothing to gain by helping me, but they did it anyway. I grew accustomed to receiving the help and support of my family, my network of mentors, and all those angels I've met along the way. In the current vernacular, it was all about me. I admit that I never spent much time putting myself in anyone else's shoes. I never thought about the sacrifices Coach Mack made for me, or the time it took out of Dr. Lewes's day to help me. I simply took their graciousness and kindness and used it to my advantage.

I was a needy child, a needy adolescent, and still needy well into adulthood. I was still learning what it means to give and what giving meant to those who gave so much to me.

I certainly can't fault my mother for failing to set an example. If ever there was a call for volunteers at our church, Clarice would volunteer not only her time but that of her children. If there was a family gathering at someone's house, she expected the Pitts children to help set up chairs and tables and break them down afterward. "Helping hands please God," she'd often say. Countless times she would make room for "one more" at our dinner table. Sometimes it was one of her clients from work; another time it would be a teenage mother or a homeless person. Like plenty of social workers and teachers, my mother saw her job as a calling that extended beyond the office or office hours. My mother always said that when we open our arms wide to give away the gifts we have, that only creates room for God to give us more. Serving others, she always taught us, is a valued virtue.

But in the midst of my own overwhelming needs, I lost the time and energy to extend compassion. I was too busy trying to fix my own flaws. It wasn't until I witnessed extraordinary acts of kindness by my colleagues and by those we met, many of them in remote corners of the world, that I began to actually look back and appreciate the sacrifices people had made in my life. Most of what I've seen has only reinforced the lessons I learned as a boy. Most people are good. Whether it's somewhere in the United States or some faraway place, there are always people willing to make a sacrifice for others. Countless acts of kindness go on every day somewhere on earth. Some of the most rewarding acts

I witnessed came from people who didn't really have the means or the time to help someone else, but they did it anyway. People who all had a willingness to step out beyond what might have been expected of them, and as a result they demonstrated amazing kindness. As I see it, they stepped out on a faith in something greater than themselves.

IN AFGHANISTAN

Our team saw many horrible and violent things in Afghanistan that fall of 2001. But we also saw the goodness that lives inside. As I traveled from northern Afghanistan toward Kabul with producer Larry Doyle and cameraman Mark Laganga, we met bandits and beggars and one remarkable family. We met them in Khoja Bahauddin in northern Afghanistan, where they were forced to flee after the Taliban took over their home city. The Nazir family, a husband and wife with two children, were almost like a typical American family. Always well groomed, they had an air of confidence that especially stood out in Afghanistan, where so many people walked around covered in dust, with rounded shoulders and heads bowed seemingly with the burdens of the world. (I met an Afghan man early on in my visit, who, before I spoke, sized me up and said, "You're an American." I smiled and asked what made him so certain, considering that I could be African or European. He said, "You walk like an American, with long strides and your head in the air.") Every member of this family walked like Americans, especially the children. The parents were a hardworking, handsome couple whose primary goal was that universal desire to provide a better life for their kids.

Fahranaz, the mother, was a Soviet-trained electrical engineer, and so was her husband, Nazir. Their teenage son, Kambiz, had dark hair and teen-idol looks. He spoke English so well he became one of our interpreters. The daughter, Vida, who was probably about seven years old, was as precious as any child you could meet and always underfoot asking questions about the world beyond her own or toying with our television equipment. This one family in particular reminded all of us of our own families back in the States and the heavy toll war takes on loved ones caught in the midst of it.

After careful discussion with Nazir, Fahranaz, and our producer Larry Doyle, it was agreed that the family would be relatively safe with us. This was a presumption based simply on one rule of war, that there is usually safety in numbers. So Larry put them on the payroll. They were worth every penny. Nazir was a gifted engineer, who kept our equipment in tiptop shape despite limited access to replacement parts and a steady source of electricity. Not to mention the dust and sand that would constantly get inside the equipment. Mishaps that would send the average engineer back in the States on an angry tirade just made Nazir smile more broadly. Fahranaz was also a tremendous resource. She often pointed us in the right direction for a story or contacts. She provided access into an underground network of women who desperately wanted their voices heard but who were forced to balance their taste for freedom with the day-to-day struggle of staying alive. Back in Kabul, Fahranaz had been active in women's rights organizations before the Taliban took over. In Khoja Bahauddin, she was still doing activist work with women, running literacy programs and postnatal care seminars. Despite all the discourse about freedom from the Taliban in the north, the local warlords did not like Fahranaz teaching women about their rights. Soon there was the strong suggestion that some in the area wanted her dead.

To escape the threat, they traveled with our team for part of the trip south, but eventually the journey became too hectic and too dangerous for a family to keep up the pace. They stayed behind in a village where they would be safe. The Nazirs were always resourceful; they assured us they would be fine. When it reached the time to say good-bye, I thought that's what it meant. On this trip, like so many others, we had met people, depended on one another, lived together, and enjoyed an intense but brief relationship. Especially with the local population, good-bye usually meant forever.

Yet despite our twenty-hour days and our own adventures on the road, Larry stayed in touch with the Nazir family, as did another one of my colleagues, correspondent Elizabeth Palmer. Elizabeth did several tours in Afghanistan and worked with the Nazir family. When she returned home to London, she stayed in contact. It was a relationship Larry and Elizabeth nurtured long distance by phone, fax machines, handwritten notes delivered by strangers from one village to the next, messages passed along by word of mouth, and by what remains the most reliable source of communication around the world—cash put in the right hands. More than a relationship, the family's security had become a cause for Larry and Elizabeth. For more than a year they kept track of this one family with one goal in mind: to help them make a better life for their children.

In time, Larry and Elizabeth, with help from a network of friends and contacts around the world, managed to get Nazir and his wife and children out of Afghanistan. Today, they live in Canada. Their son is in medical school. Their daughter, as Elizabeth describes her, is a typical Canadian teenager. It says a great deal about Larry and Elizabeth. They helped a family they might have left behind. I asked them both why, and both agreed that it was because it needed to be done. They helped someone simply because it needed to be done.

Elizabeth added, "I liked them. I thought they were extraordinarily brave and honest. I think when such opportunities present themselves, it's important to grab them."

Few people inside *CBS News* ever knew what Larry and Elizabeth were up to. They spent their own time and their own money and sought nothing in return. It was not about winning an award, receiving special recognition, or even getting a story on the *CBS Evening News*. For them, it was more than that, it was about making a difference. They used their own gifts and gave them away. Who knows what a Canadian doctor born in Afghanistan will do someday? Look out, world, when Vida pursues her dreams.

Here's a footnote to the story. It almost never happened. When Larry first approached Fahranaz about her son working as an interpreter for CBS, she said no. She was afraid it was a trick to get her son to fight for the Taliban. That kind of watchful paranoia keeps people safe in wartime. Larry and Elizabeth were able to do their good work because they refused to take no for an answer.

THE FALL OF BAGHDAD

Just days after the U.S. military invaded Iraq in 2003, the nation was given a sense of hope that the war would be brief. Most Americans woke on April 9 to images of Iraqis celebrating in the streets of Baghdad, as many of their countrymen pulled down and kicked a statue of Saddam Hussein in the middle of the city. That impression did not last long. I was a few blocks away from the celebration, along with Mark Laganga. We were embedded with the U.S. Marine Corps Lima Company out of Twentynine Palms, California. The embed program was put in place by the Pentagon after lengthy discussion about the best way to give major news organizations (and their audiences) the fullest and most unfiltered access to the war. The program would be widely criticized later on. But in the early days and weeks of the war, it gave America a front-row seat to war.

On this particular morning, *CBS News* gave viewers a split screen of the war. On one side, there were the hopeful images from downtown Baghdad of the capital city of Iraq apparently under the control of U.S. forces. On the other side of the screen and a few blocks away, U.S. Marines were engaged in an all-out firefight.

Earlier in the day, the Marines of Lima Company were assigned to clear the Iraqi Ministry of Oil building. They were cautioned to be on the lookout for snipers. Mark and I tagged along, actually hoping to see what was commonly referred to as "bang bang," American troops engaging the enemy. The early minutes of the mission were tense but uneventful. The Marines methodically went floor by floor looking for snipers or Iraqi fighters. Mark and I followed. We had been together for nearly six months by this time. We started our duty in Kuwait, where the buildup to the war began. By now Mark and I knew almost instinctively the other's movements and thought process. We could communicate without ever exchanging a word. So we split up that morning in order to cover more ground. Mark with his large network camera and me with a small digital video variety, the kind you would take to Disney World. It was one of the few days of my life I hated being over six feet tall. Besides being the oldest person with the group of Marines, I was just about the tallest. My fear was that I was an easy target, and at age forty-two I had the disadvantage of being a bit slow, alongside the twenty-something Marines. But it appeared that all of my anxiety was for naught. The building was safe.

An hour or so after storming the Oil Ministry, the Marines gathered on the front steps to catch their breath. Some rested. A few pulled out cigars. The day was almost over, and no one had fired a weapon. Our reverie ended with the crackle of gunfire and falling debris. In a war zone, the sound of gunfire begins to blend in with the background. We realized there was a problem only when plaster from the building overhead was starting to falling on our heads. "Holy shit," a Marine yelled. Someone was shooting at us. Everyone scrambled for cover. For weeks leading up to this moment, Mark and I had trained and studied with the Marines on how to respond to a chemical weapons attack, an air raid, trench warfare, and first aid. I do not recall a lesson on what to do in a firefight on the concrete in downtown Baghdad, so I got as low to the ground as I could and tried to keep up with the Marines in front of me.

While Mark videotaped the action, I placed a call to the New York office on our satellite phone to offer a live report. The first time I dialed in, a young person answered the phone. Sounded like one of the recent grads assigned to work the early shift back in New York. The person yelled into the phone, "I can't hear you; there's too much noise in the background." And they hung up. I looked at the satellite phone in disbelief. I wanted to curse, but there was no time. The Marines were about to change position. It was time to run. I was teamed up with a corporal and one of the company's staff sergeants. The corporal was young, thin, and athletic. The sergeant was just a bit younger than I, barrel-chested, with the classic Marine Corps tough-guy demeanor. I felt safe in his presence. The goal was to cross the outdoor mall beside the Ministry of Oil and make it to the wall surrounding the building. Run, stay low, then run again was the basic strategy. If cover was a necessity, there were cement tables scattered about. I imagined that workers in more peaceful times at the ministry might have sat outside at one of the tables enjoying their lunch. At the moment we would use the tables as temporary shelters. Somehow, the three of us—the corporal, the sergeant, and I—eyed the same cement table. The corporal got there first and the sergeant was a close second. I had the least amount of gear (flak jacket, helmet, small camera, satellite phone, and a notebook) but moved the slowest.

With no place safe to land, I dove on the sergeant's back—not intentionally—but I wasn't planning on moving right away either.

With gunfire above our heads, I buried my face in the back of the sergeant's neck, like a schoolgirl at her first horror movie. I wasn't particularly scared, mind you, but the sergeant was my security blanket and I was determined to stay wrapped up as long as I could. It was only a few seconds I'm certain, but it felt like much longer. As the gunfire temporarily subsided, the sergeant twisted his neck toward me. If not for our helmets, we would have been cheek to cheek.

In a calm voice inconsistent with the panic I was feeling, he asked me, "Are you okay? Are you bleeding? Any wet spots?"

I quickly did a hand check and fired back, "No, sir, sergeant! I'm fine."

In that same calm voice, he answered, "Are you sure?"

I answered, "Yes, sir, I'm fine."

Then, after a brief pause, perhaps for effect, the sergeant cleared his throat and in a very matter-of-fact tone said, "Okay, then fuck me or get off of me. But you can't just lay there."

If I had been eating, I would have spit out my food. He had detected tension in my voice and wanted to both reassure me and ease the mood. It worked. I sheepishly apologized, rolled to the side, and the three of us got up and ran to safety behind a wall. By now I had reconnected with the CBS office and was filing minute-by-minute reports to the control room for broadcast in New York. We did not have live pictures, only the sound of my voice describing the action, punctuated by bursts of gunfire and the shouting voices of the Marines around me. The gunfire aimed in our direction had not abated. The enemy was still an invisible target. In the midst of all the chaos came a moment I will remember the rest of my life. It was minor in the scheme of things, but it spoke volumes to me about the character of most of the men and women the American government sent into harm's way.

Lima Company was led by Captain George Schreffler from Harrisburg, Pennsylvania. He had the temperament of Tom Hanks in the movie *Saving Private Ryan*. His demeanor was often more professorial than warrior. Captain Schreffler was as calm as the quarterback in a church league flag football game, coolly calling out plays. Surrounded by a few of his Marines, including his radioman, he directed the movement of his unit and coordinated the call for support. A Marine corporal rushed over to tell the captain that his men had located the source of the gunfire. The corporal answered that he was certain of the location but could not confirm the identity of those firing. I for one was relieved by the news, but Captain Schreffler did not seem impressed. He instructed the Marine that no one was allowed to fire at the position in question until the threat was properly identified. I felt deflated by his strict instructions. We were getting pounded by gunfire, and I did not understand why he was reluctant to take out the target. But we soon realized that Captain Schreffler had made the correct call. He had been patient and protective of both his men and the potential enemy. It turned out that objects moving in the distance, once identified earlier as the source of the incoming fire, were actually members of an Iraqi family caught in the crossfire. If Captain Schreffler had given permission to shoot, that family would almost certainly have been killed.

Here's how I described those hours that night.

The CBS Evening News, April 9, 2003

This morning the U.S. Marines rolled into downtown Baghdad . . . locked and loaded for a fight . . . when a party broke out.

Iraqi citizens chanting and screaming as they tore down this life-size statue of Saddam Hussein . . . on the steps of the Iraqi Oil Ministry . . . as the Marines were clearing this thirteen-story building. It was one of the last remaining symbols of Saddam's regime.

Iraqi citizen: *"We hate Saddam! Thank you USA!"*

Staff Sergeant, USMC: *"I wish it was him they were tearing down, but the statue is nice."*

Lieutenant, USMC: *"You know we've been fighting for days and to see this let's us know the Iraqi people are glad we're here, and maybe we're going home."*

But suddenly the celebration stopped with the crackle of gunfire. The party ended when these Marines were ambushed from three sides.

This wasn't warfare. This was a street fight. U.S. Marines . . . average age nineteen to twenty-two . . . each with an M-16 . . . versus Saddam's Fedayen paramilitary . . . also young men . . . with AK 47s.

Nearly two hours of small-arms fire . . . and rocket-propelled grenade launches. These Marines from Lima Company . . . based in Twentynine Palms, California, are flanked on three sides by sniper fire . . . when a corporal spots three heads bobbing behind a wall. He pleads with Lima Company's commanding officer to take the shot. But Captain George Scheffler from Harrisburg, Pennsylvania, orders his man to stand down. Wait until he can see a weapon. The captain made the right call. Those three heads were an Iraqi family—a husband, his wife, and daughter.

In the end, there were two Iraqi snipers dead . . . a third escaped. No American casualties. And a platoon of young Marines learned a valuable lesson: America is winning this war, but she cannot end it, at least not yet. Byron Pitts, CBS News, Baghdad.

It was the most "bang, bang" I would see for quite a while. That night I unwound for a few hours with Mark and the captain. He walked us through the day's events. I was both curious and amazed by his calmness and clarity earlier in the day when so much was going on. "It's what I was trained to do," he said, without even a hint of arrogance or bravado. "I'm here to do a job. I'm not here to kill anyone I don't have to kill," he added.

Before we said our good nights, Captain Schreffler added, "I love my family, the Marine Corps, and my country. I would never do anything to dishonor them."

There were plenty of well-publicized low moments during the war in Iraq, moments that deserved the attention they received. I only wish moments like the one I witnessed the day Baghdad fell would have gotten more attention.

Acts of courage, decency, and humility often go unnoticed, and not just on the battlefield.

HURRICANE MITCH

On October 29, 1998, category five Hurricane Mitch with 180-mile-an-hour winds hit the Central American countries of Honduras and Nicaragua. Over the next six days, the hurricane dumped a record seventy-five inches of rain, causing catastrophic flooding, killing nearly 11,000 people; another 11,000 were missing, and 2.7 million were left homeless. The damage was estimated at $5 billion. It was the second deadliest Atlantic hurricane in history. Those statistics provide the wide shot. For the closeup *CBS News* dispatched nearly the entire Miami bureau. That meant producer Larry Doyle, cameraman Manny Alvarez, soundman Craig Anderson, and me. We were a small office staff with eighty-two years of network experience combined. I provided the last two years. Manny is a Cuban-American who has the best sense of humor of anyone I have ever worked with. He can mix humor and sarcasm better than Larry can mix a drink. Larry had his rules for the road, and so did Manny. Never stand when you can sit. Never sit when you can lie down, and never just lie down when you can sleep. And a favorite of many a profession: eat when you can, as often as you can, because you never know when you will get your next meal. And then there is Craig Anderson. Built like a tank with the patience of Job, he has one of the best B.S. meters in television. Nothing got by Craig, and no one got one over on him.

Like many of these assignments, there was no road map. The assignment was to get on the ground as soon as we could and start sending in reports. We filed our first report along the Choluteca River in the city of Tegucigalpa, the capital of Honduras. The grim statistics that sent us to Honduras in the first place were mere echoes to the horror stories we heard on the ground. Survivors had poured into Tegucigalpa from villages miles away, with just the clothes on their backs. Many told of losing their entire families. Some set up make-shift tent cities along the river. Children were swimming and women washing clothes along one stretch of the river, while men, women, and children were relieving themselves along another portion. The place was rife with disease.

A few days into our trip, we traveled by small propeller plane and then by boat to remote parts of northern Honduras. We almost became part of the story. Never a big fan of flying, I was particularly uncomfortable in small planes. In a developing country after a major natural disaster, cash can get you only so much, so Larry rented the only plane available. It was a small twin-engine plane that could hold six people, including pilot and co-pilot. Larry, Manny, Craig, and I made four. After exaggerating about the weight of our gear and two additional Benjamin Franklins, the crew agreed to take us to a remote part of Honduras. We all assumed our usual positions: Manny in his own world, fussing over his gear; Craig and I talking about anything other than work; and Larry asleep in the back of the plane. As Manny was videotaping out the window of the plane and Craig and I were enjoying the view, we heard a loud noise. It sounded like flesh smashing together. We looked forward to see the co-pilot slapping the pilot for the second time. Neither Manny, Craig, or I had ever flown a plane, but we knew enough to figure out something was wrong. The pilot and co-pilot were screaming at each other in Spanish. Manny quickly filled in the gaps. The pilot was watching Manny videotaping, instead of watching his instruments. We were heading directly into the side of a mountain. The co-pilot slapped the pilot to gain his attention. The pilot pulled hard on the control, and the nose of the plane pointed skyward. Now we were all scream-ing, except for Larry who was still sound asleep. We barely cleared the mountain. When we landed, Manny, Craig, and I were still shaking and were soaked in sweat. Larry asked what was wrong. When we explained, he smiled and said, "Glad you didn't wake me."

There was plenty of death to be seen in the days that fol-lowed. Whole towns had vanished beneath the mud. We saw survivors living in trees and on slivers of land barely above water. In one place called Waller, we met Vicenta Lopez and her four children. She was twenty-eight but looked nearly fifty. Her oldest child was twelve, and the baby was barely old enough to walk. The family was practically homeless, except for a thin tin roof leaning against a stack of fallen trees, beneath which they slept and ate. She and her children were poor before the storm, but Hurricane Mitch had taken what little they had. Inside their makeshift home were three small stools, which the children used as chairs, a small table not much larger than a manhole cover, a few plastic bowls, cups, spoons, and one wooden spoon. A few days earlier an international charity working in the area provided Miss Lopez with rice and a large container of fresh water. She had a small fire burning just outside. Dinner that night for her and her children would consist of plain white rice.

Manny spoke to her in Spanish and asked her permission to videotape her preparation for dinner and the children sitting down to eat. She smiled and nodded yes. But then she did something that surprised us all. "Por favor [please]," she said in Spanish, "eat with us." She invited us to sit down with her family for dinner. Actually, she insisted. In a translated back and forth, we begged for them to eat without us. We were four healthy grown men who twenty-four hours earlier had slept in a hotel and had had three hot meals. Besides that, in about a week we would be back in our comfortable homes and comfortable lives.

Larry tried to seize control. "Let's go," he said, and the four of us backed up. "No! No! No!" she shot back as she moved to block our way. Wearing a worn apron around her waist, she used the edges to dust off the small table. She waved for her children to make room. With gap-toothed smiles and their almond-shaped eyes focused on us, they moved their small stools closer together to make room for their guests. Larry, Manny, Craig, and I all had tears in our eyes. I knew Larry was easy to tear up. Manny is passionate about most things, but Craig isn't. He was always the coolest member of our team. But the moment had even gotten to him. "Damn," Craig muttered under his breath. "I thought these things weren't supposed to get to us," as he wiped his eyes. This family had as close to nothing as almost any family you could imagine, and they desperately wanted to share. We were the American journalists who had come to this faraway place to tell the world of a horrific natural disaster and perhaps in some way help families like the Lopezes. And this poor woman with not even enough to properly feed herself and her children was offering to share with us. Finally, she relented and the family began to eat, a fistful of rice apiece. The gesture alone left our whole team emotionally spent for the rest of the day. We tried offering her some of our bottled water and some supplies, but she declined, though Manny did convince her to take our empty plastic water bottles so she could use them later to transport water back to her children. There must be a place reserved in heaven for people like Vicenta Lopez.

It's been my great joy to meet people with Vicenta's same spirit right here at home in the United States.

THE NOTHING STORM

Some of the most remarkable things I have witnessed occurred in what some might describe as less than memorable or significant occasions. I guess it is all about perspective.

Meaux, Louisiana, is a spit of a town along the Louisiana coast. It is a speck on the map twenty miles southwest of Lafayette. In fact, you likely will not find it on most maps.

It's like my mother's hometown of Friendship, North Carolina.
You normally go there for one of two reasons. Either you are
visiting family or you're lost. I was traveling with *CBS News*
producer Betty Chin on October 3, 2002, when Hurricane
Lili hit the Gulf Coast. It was supposed to have been a major
hurricane, but fortunately the winds died down, and Lili
made landfall as a category one hurricane. To the bosses in
New York, it was no big deal. When the morning began,
Betty and I had the lead story in the broadcast. By lunchtime,
our executive producer pulled the plug. Betty and I were
given permission to head home, and most days that would
have been the end of it. Hurricane duty usually means long
days, little sleep, and bad food on top of the awful weather
conditions and the sad stories you come across. Without the
lead story, Betty and I were heading toward New Orleans for
a decent meal, a nice hotel, and a good night's sleep before flying out the next day. We just happened to drive through
Meaux. We were lost. Betty and I have probably logged more
miles lost than almost any other correspondent and producer
team at the network. My fault. Fortunately, Betty is incredibly
good-natured, and we have always made the best of it. We
weren't looking for a story in Meaux; the story found us. We
had been in the car for hours and had not seen much storm
damage when we saw a man standing in an open field littered
with trash and a pile of debris on Abshire Road in Meaux. His
arms were full of garbage, and he had a big smile on his face.
He looked out of place. We wondered why this man looked so
cheery when the weather was so lousy. Betty and I decided to
stop and ask. We also thought he might direct us to the nearest gas station or at least get us back to the highway.

"Hi ya'll doin" is the way Jim Williams greeted us. He looked to be in his late twenties, an athletic young man with a cheery disposition. Come to find out he was a lieutenant in the National Guard. His unit had been assigned to help with storm rescue and cleanup. Since there was more cleanup than rescue needed, his commanding officer let him slip away for a bit to check on his own home. It was gone. That open field was Jim's yard. The trash and pile of debris scattered about was all that was left of his house. By history's high standard, hurricane Lili was a lightweight. But it was enough to destroy Jim Williams's home and leave him, his wife, and his three children homeless. Fortunately, Jim's family had gone to stay with relatives while he was assigned Guard duty. I asked him what he thought might have happened if they had all been at home when the storm hit.

"Boy, just looking at it, I'd be at the hospital or at the morgue right now, one or the other," he said, still smiling and with sweat gathering at the bottom of his chin.

Betty and I, along with our crew, helped him find a few valuables buried in what used to be the master bedroom. He found a few pictures and the family Bible. He seemed satisfied, like a man who had just eaten a good meal or finished building a bookcase by hand. Why appear so hopeful? I asked him.

"I have faith—that's just all it is. I can't attribute it to anything else but just saying, All right, God's not going to give you anything you can't handle, so, you know, I just wish He didn't trust me so much, you know," and his smile even broadened.

We spent about an hour with Jim Williams. The only time

his spirits appeared to falter was when he talked about his children. "It makes you want to cry when your four-year-old goes to your wife, her mom, and says, 'Mama, why are you crying,' " he said.

I have covered plenty of disasters, and you can always tell when someone has been crying. It did not appear that Jim Williams ever shed a tear. He thanked us for our help, and then said he had to leave soon. He was going back to his National Guard unit. "There are people who fared far worse than us, and they need our help," he said.

In reality, the Williams family had lost nearly as much as any family in Meaux. That did not seem to matter to Jim because he had a job to do. He cheerfully put the needs of others ahead of his own. As we pulled out of his driveway, Jim Williams was smiling and waving. He looked as if he didn't have a care in the world. We thought we had found a some-thing story in this nothing storm. We pleaded with the executives in New York, and about an hour before the broadcast, they dropped another story and made room. Betty and I told the world about Jim Williams on the *CBS Evening News* that night. Funny, the wonderful golden nuggets God can lead you to when you are lost, with open eyes and outstretched arms.

THE HUG DOCTOR WHO MAKES HOUSE CALLS

Dr. Regina Benjamin is one of the most beloved physicians in southern Alabama, partly because, for the longest time, she was one of the few. Dr. Benjamin runs a medical clinic in

Bayou La Batre, Alabama. She was just one of the many people I profiled for the *CBS Evening News* in stories about the recovery underway along the Gulf Coast after 2005's Hurricane Katrina. When I met her, she had 4,000 patients. You read right, 4,000 patients. And she made house calls. She drove an average of 300 miles per week across rural Alabama's shrimp country. She pulled fish hooks out of patients, delivered babies, and stabilized weak hearts. She had long days before Hurricane Katrina devastated the Gulf Coast. Her days got even longer in the months afterward. By some estimates, nearly 6,000 physicians were displaced from the region after Katrina. The hurricane flooded Dr. Benjamin's clinic. The following New Year's Day, the clinic caught fire and burned down. She stayed and rebuilt it. I asked her why not just close up shop and leave. She was a highly trained physician, a minority, and could practically name her price someplace else. She had a quick answer.

"This is my place. This is my price," she said without an ounce of regret, in fact, with a bit of an edge. Most people are fond of their primary-care physician. Dr. Benjamin's patients said they loved her. Everyone I spoke with used that word, *love*. Stan White, the mayor of Bayou La Batre, called her "the lifeblood of our community," adding, "I don't think we could survive without her." Certainly any number of people in the area would not have access to health care without her. Her clinic charged seven dollars per visit. Any treatments not covered by Medicare or Medicaid, Dr. Benjamin paid out of her own pocket or with federal grant money. She even dispensed hugs, as did her nurse. The patients affectionately refer to Nurse Nell Stoddard as Granny. She described the clinic this way: "We're a hugging office. We hug everybody. We'll hug you if you want to be hugged." And she did. I can count on one hand the number of times I've been hugged on a story in twenty-five years of reporting.

Dr. Benjamin talked a great deal about the character of her patients, especially the ones who could not afford to pay even the seven dollars. They lack money not pride, she said. They pay what they can when they can. More than just taking care of their health needs, it seemed that Dr. Benjamin was in the business of restoring her patients' dignity. She insisted she was well compensated.

"To know you made a difference, when a mother smiles after you tell her her baby is going to be okay. There's nothing like it," she said, smiling herself. "I've got the greatest job in the world," she said.

I agree with Dr. Benjamin. I feel the same about my job. It's allowed me to see my share of evil around the world, but it has also brought focus to the compassionate and caring spirit of so many. I can't look at my life now without recognizing that I too was once one of the "least of us" to whom so many reached out their hands. I won't live long enough to either repay those who've given so much to me or pay it forward. But it will keep me busy and always grateful. As for Regina Benjamin, in 2009, President Obama nominated the hug doctor to be surgeon general of the United States.

TWELVE

The Power of Prayer and Optimism

God *is* my strength *and* power; And he maketh my way perfect.

—2 Samuel 22:33

As I became one of the more senior correspondents at *CBS News*, people began seeking my opinion and my advice. Everyone from college students to up-and-coming young journalists, even established reporters and peers. They sought me out for encouragement and career counsel. For the longest time it seemed strange to me because I had always been the dependent one, in need of mentoring. I didn't consider my life or my career to be a model for anyone to follow. But I certainly saw this opportunity as one way to give back some of the time and attention I had been given. If I had the power to influence other people's lives, I needed to fully understand the source of my own strength. It took me more than forty years, but I was finally beginning to understand where my own power came from. One important factor was patience, the willingness to wait for my opportunities but remain productive in the meantime. As Coach John Wooden said, "Be quick, but don't hurry." As I've mentioned, long before I started at *CBS News*, the goal was to report for *60 Minutes*. It was my equivalent of the professional gold ring. Once at the network, I had to build a body of work and a reputation to get there, or at least get myself the chance. My prayer had never been "Lord, put me on *60 Minutes* someday." It was always just "Lord make me good enough to one day have the chance."

Not long after I moved to New York, I made it my business to find out where the *60 Minutes* offices were located. The staff works in a different building from the rest of *CBS News*. On lunch breaks, quiet days, and just for a change of scenery, I'd cross the street and make my way over to *60 Minutes*, where I'd see some of the most powerful figures in broadcast news: Mike Wallace, Morley Safer, Lesley Stahl, and Steve Kroft. Later, Bob Simon, Scott Pelley, and Katie Couric. I can still remember watching Ed Bradley gliding down the hallways. Ed made cool look good. I knew a few people who worked there, but I rarely stopped by their offices. I really just wanted to get a feel for the place, like a minor leaguer getting his first chance to walk around the field at Yankee Stadium. While some CBS staffers would walk down the street, smoke a cigarette, or go to the park to clear their head, I'd roam the hallways of *60 Minutes*. Long ago, when I overcame illiteracy, I discovered I needed to visualize things, have a snapshot in my mind of what I wanted to accomplish and where I wanted to be. I'd walk by the correspondents' offices just to peek in and see what they were doing and imagine myself there. That may sound childish, but remember I spent hours of my life staring into a bath-room mirror holding a toothbrush. Much to my relief, the *60 Minutes* guys were rarely around. I was often just staring at stacks of books and awards that lined their bookshelves. When they were in, I'd observe them buried in a book, crouched over a computer screen, scribbling notes, or con-ferring with a colleague. As a visual learner, I also spent a lot of time studying their video clips, watching how they con-ducted their interviews, how they interacted with their inter-view subjects. I carry a pretty good library of *60 Minutes* stories in my head. I knew I could only get to *60 Minutes* if I could see *60 Minutes* and put myself in the space. There is power in having the patience to visualize your path.

I've spent a good bit of my career covering power. The power of nature and the power of man to do good and cause harm. Still, the greatest forces I've ever experienced can't be captured by a television camera, just felt in the bones. As a Christian, I was raised to believe in other powerful forces, things that have become sources of both strength and com-fort. These are all small things in size. You could fit them in a shirt pocket. I've come to believe they are fundamental to my strength: the power of prayer, the power of optimism, and, on more than a few occasions, the power of laughter.

I can't think of a single major decision I make without praying about it. I may seek the advice of my family, my friends, even respected colleagues, but I won't make a final decision until I've prayed. I have always believed that God could fill the gap between what I wanted to do and what was right for me to do—from my desperate prayers as a child for the ability to read to prayers for protection under dangerous circumstances. The war in Iraq tested the power of prayer in my life.

I've always prided myself on being physically and mentally prepared for every major assignment I've been sent on. I was part of the first wave of embedded journalists trained at the Quantico Marine Corps base in Virginia in December 2002 as the United States moved toward war in Iraq. We ran, hiked, exercised, and took crash courses in first aid, chemical weapons, and explosives. It gave all of us who participated a sense of what we might face overseas. It was the third war-training program I had attended. To prepare myself physically for the war, I also took five-mile walks around my hometown carrying forty pounds in a backpack to strengthen my back and toughen my feet. With flashlights, batteries, Band-Aids, a sleeping bag, and a big bottle of Tabasco sauce, I left for Kuwait in January 2003. I'd learned over the years that Tabasco sauce could make anything taste better, or at the very least mask the taste of whatever I was eating.

Most of us on assignment covering the buildup to war gathered at the Sheraton Hotel in Kuwait. From there, we could go back and forth into the desert where U.S. troops were massing at the Iraq border and still be back at the hotel in time for happy hour. Cameraman Mark Laganga and I teamed up and eventually joined a Marine Corps attack helicopter squadron in late February. The second Gulf War officially started on March 20, 2003. I was away from home for nearly six months. When my tour was over, I came back to the States hoping not to have to return to Iraq any time soon. Boy, was I wrong. I went back to Iraq twice more in less than two years. The first time, I was home for about two months when my bosses asked me to go back again. By that time, there wasn't a long line of journalists raising their hands for bureau duty in Baghdad at any of the networks, including *CBS News*. It was certainly understandable. It was dangerous and dirty work, but I took the assignment. I was still in pretty good shape and the dynamics of the war hadn't changed dramatically. After a month in Iraq, I was back in the States.

With the violence and the death toll in Iraq escalating in March 2005, and the United States deeply entrenched in battle, our executives were once again asking for volunteers to go into Baghdad. It had been nearly two years since I'd come home from Iraq the first time. I didn't volunteer, but when a colleague scheduled for Baghdad duty got sick, CBS needed a quick replacement. Reluctantly I stepped forward. "Reluctant" because I knew that I wasn't prepared physically or emotionally to go. With a week to get ready, there was no time for my exercise routine and no time to read all the briefing material on the war to that point. The weekend before I was to travel, I was more nervous than I had been that first trip. This time I knew the risks. Kidnappings, roadside bombs, and snipers abounded. Even the seven-and-a-half-mile trip from the Baghdad airport to the center of the city was treacherous, nicknamed Ambush Alley.

That Sunday I went to church with my wife and children. I did my best to put on a good face for the family. Besides, church was always a place of great comfort. After church, a group of deacons called me up front for prayer. A nice gesture, I thought, prayer is always a good thing. But this would be a new experience for me. The deacons, both male and female, placed me in the middle of a circle. They each put their hands on me, at least a half dozen people with their hands placed on my shoulders, chest, and arms. I admit to being a little uncomfortable at first. I'd certainly seen a number of prayer circles over the years, but this was the first time I had been in the middle of one.

One of the church ministers, Reverend Joseph Andrews, joined the circle. He did something that really made me uncomfortable: he put both his hands on my head. Since I'm an inch or two taller than Reverend Andrews, he really had to stretch to place both hands up there. Just before we all closed our eyes, I caught a glimpse of Reverend Andrews and he had a big smile on his face. Reverend Andrews has a booming voice, even in regular conversation. One by one, the deacons each gave a short prayer, asking God to keep me safe in Iraq and to keep my family safe and worry-free while I was away. The whole time Reverend Andrews kept his hands pressing against the top of my head. He prayed last. "Lord," he said with his Trinidadian accent, "be with our brother over in Iraq. Give him traveling mercy. And, Lord, let no harm come to him from the top of his head to the bottom of his feet."

When he finished, I felt a bit embarrassed for being so uncomfortable. But, more important, I felt a tremendous sense of peace. I could still feel Reverend Andrews's hands on my head and the hands of the deacons. I walked over to my family, standing in the back of the church, with a look of complete contentment. I may not have been quite up to Iraq physically, but I was, as military people are fond of saying, "high speed and good to go." I was ready spiritually.

Often, during the plane rides from New York to London,

London to Amman, Jordan, and Amman to Baghdad, I thought about that small prayer group. Security protocol called for a small private security team to meet me just outside the Baghdad airport. It was made up of three armed men traveling in two vehicles. There was one driver and two armed guards in one car, and then me with one armed guard and driver in the other. The drivers were all trained to maneuver in traffic and to take evasive action in case of attack. It was a high-speed sprint from the airport to the hotel CBS used as its headquarters. But this was an uneventful trip until we got there. Just as we were about to enter the secured gates around the hotel, we heard a loud bang. I could see people in the hotel courtyard running and diving for cover. The security guard in the front passenger seat ordered me to get down. I was already wearing a Kevlar vest, but I knew not to challenge him at that moment. Our car accelerated a short distance and then stopped abruptly. "Out of the car, mate, into the hotel straightaway," the British-born security guard yelled. Our hotel had just been hit by at least two mortars. One exploded and one did not. I wish I could say I started praying, but instead I asked God a question, "Lord, already? I just got here." I didn't wait for an answer—I ran for the hotel lobby. The unexploded ordnance was now resting on the ground outside the hotel. There's a good chance that if that mortar had gone off, shrapnel would have sprayed the courtyard and most likely hit the car I was in. "Boy, were you guys lucky," CBS producer Ben Plesser said, with his hand outstretched. "Welcome to Baghdad," he added with a smile. Perhaps we were lucky, but that's not how I saw it. For the next few minutes, my mind went back to my friends at St. Paul Baptist Church, who stood around me in a circle and prayed. I could feel their hands, especially Reverend Andrews's hands on my head and hear his words "from the top of his head to the bottom of his feet." When we settled upstairs in the hotel in the *CBS News* work space, Ben said with a hint of surprise, "You seemed awfully calm for a guy who almost got nailed by a mortar." My response was honest, "Not calm, just prayed up," I said. Later that night, when I finally went to bed, I again thought about that prayer circle. I slept like a baby.

It was, by the standards of war, a relatively uneventful month-long tour in Baghdad. We saw some "bang bang," as journalists are fond of saying, but no real close calls. Nonbelievers will contend those prayers had nothing to do with how things turned out. If safety and prayer were that easily tied together, why have so many people died in Iraq and elsewhere? My short answer is, I don't know. I do know the prayers of those friends comforted me the way prayers I had heard my mother and grandmother and others utter over the years. Prayers that remind us that whatever the eventual outcome, God will have a hand in it. When my mother prays, she often says, "Lord, not my will but Yours be done." That humble request has always worked for me.

I believe prayer works best when uttered from the bent knees of an optimist. A minister friend asked me once if my cup was half full or half empty. I stuck my chest out and proclaimed half full. His response was startling, Why are you optimistic only half of the time, he asked. Why not be optimistic all the time? Why not say your cup is constantly running over? That's always struck me as an awfully tall order.

Is it possible to be optimistic all the time? Over the years my life's been touched by a handful of people who have that kind of optimism, and they have helped me recognize and increase my own spirit of optimism. We all believe in putting the best face on a difficult circumstance and in anticipating the best possible outcome. We choose to be optimistic. At her core, my mother is one of these optimists. Despite what my grades showed or what a psychologist said, she believed my cup was running over, that I could do great things with my life. Optimists don't allow doubt to linger or to discourage them from their goals. There is something else this group shares, and that's toughness. Optimism isn't based on any pie in the sky naiveté. It is a hard-earned choice.

I believe that kind of optimism as much as anything got me to *60 Minutes* full time in January of 2009. Sure, I worked hard, and plenty of people had to sign off on it— from the show's executive producer, Jeff Fager, to the president of *CBS News,* Sean McManus, all the way up to the president and CEO of CBS, Leslie Moonves. They all had to be in agreement. Certainly my agent, Richard Liebner, played a role in negotiating the deal. But none of that would ever have happened without the spirit of optimism that's covered my life and the silent prayers of many people. Getting to *60 Minutes* was a thrill, but staying there, that now takes up most of my energies. It's never been about the destination for me. It's all about the journey. One of the best things about being at *60 Minutes* is the amount of time devoted to a single story. Research often takes months and on occasion years. Over time there's a chance to spend hours with the people you interview. Many of them are famous and have harnessed power in their own ways. A few I've met have reinforced or taught me things far beyond their professions.

Pete Carroll is my kind of optimist. He's the head football coach at the University of Southern California. His Trojans are one of the most successful college teams in the nation. Carroll certainly collects his share of high school all-Americans and has one of the top coaching staffs in the country, but he also has one of those contagious spirits. I met Coach Carroll while doing a profile on *60 Minutes*. The story was as much about what he does outside of football as about his success on the gridiron. He's part of an effort to reduce gang violence in Los Angeles through a program he started, called A Better L.A. One night he took us along when he went to South Central Los Angeles, into several neighborhoods known for gang violence. It was well past midnight, just a few days after a big win against Ohio State. Pete's been making such visits for several years, and this was the first time he ever allowed television cameras to accompany him. He chatted with gang members and gang wannabes, and with community activists who share his desire to make L.A. a safer place. Carroll's been criticized for his work, accused of being naive and in over his head. But he laughs it off. He has also been given credit by some in law enforcement in the city for helping to reduce the level of gang violence. He believes it's possible for a person to win at whatever they put their heart and effort into, from sports to business to living their life day to day. He doesn't just believe it—he lives it. Twice he was hired as an NFL head coach, and twice he was fired. A lesser person might have just curled up in a fetal position and turned the lights out. Not Pete Carroll. He said, "Okay, let me go. Let me move on to the next thing." He processed the criticism, learned from it, and moved on, just as Clarice would have prescribed. When *60 Minutes* first approached Carroll about a profile, he was hesitant. But in the end, he decided to cooperate. Wearing his perpetual big smile, he told me off-camera before the first interview, "I'm going to trust you guys and that means I'm in." That's another quality of an optimist, a commitment to give themselves fully to things they believe in.

An optimist takes stumbling blocks and turns them into stepping stones. Dr. Paul Farmer is a living example, and that's partly why I profiled him for *60 Minutes*. He's the co-founder of a group called Partners in Health, an organization that provides medical care to poor people around the world. He divides his time between his home in Haiti and Rwanda. Paul's childhood makes mine look like a day at the beach. He was raised near Weeki Wachee, Florida (near Tampa), by working-class parents. He was one of six siblings who spent part of their childhood living on a bus. I'll repeat that: they lived on a bus. Because he grew up poor, he recognized the lack of health care and the lack of dignity associated with poverty. He had spent a lot of time in Florida with migrant workers from Haiti, so his relationship with the country was part of his early development. He went to Duke on a scholarship and later earned a medical degree at Harvard, where he committed himself to providing both quality health care and dignity.

Like most optimists, he had great clarity about his purpose in life and therefore drew great satisfaction, no matter the difficulty of the moment, in just having the opportunity to live that purpose every day. The program Dr. Farmer started in Haiti has become a model around the world for providing health care to the poor. In fact, techniques Partners in Health mastered in Haiti are being used in parts of Boston to treat poor patients in one of America's great cities. Farmer, too, has a permanent smile etched on his face. Once, when I took a flight back with him from Haiti, as we were chatting, I realized he'd stopped talking. I glanced over and he was sound asleep. He had two books open on his lap, on top of notes he was preparing for an upcoming speech. His head was tilted back, eyes closed, and there was a slight smile on his face. He's optimistic even when he's dreaming.

There is a childlike quality to many of the people whose optimistic spirits shaped my life. In addition to their optimism, they all had the ability to laugh at life and just as easily to laugh at themselves. Laughter was often a miraculous ointment for the troubles in my life. It's one of the many and most valued things I learned from my mother. "Son, sometimes you have to laugh to keep from crying," she'd say, and that's exactly what we'd do. Often at night, just before bed, I'd sit on the side of my mother's bed with my brother and sister. Some nights we'd snuggle next to her. And somehow, no matter what had occurred that day, she would find a way to make us laugh. There was no topic too sensitive or serious that we couldn't laugh at it. From her failed marriages, to difficult bosses, to her own disappointments with relationships, nothing was out of bounds. She gave each of us a great gift, the ability to laugh at ourselves. It has served me well. At times, it's been therapeutic. Other days, being able to laugh at myself or at a situation was just enough to keep me from losing control.

One of those days occurred on July 22, 2003. I was sitting in the *CBS News* office in Baghdad. It was late, and I was filling time the way I often did on this particular assignment: I was losing badly to producer Mike Solmsen at cards. Mike was a great travel companion. He could find good fried chicken anywhere in the world, talk passionately about Syracuse basketball for hours, and recite the best lines from movies like *The Godfather* and *Pulp Fiction*. All valuable skills when you can spend hours waiting at airports, on stakeouts, or like this particular night, waiting out rumors that Saddam Hussein's two sons had been killed by U.S. forces in a firefight. The rumors had been circulating for hours. We couldn't confirm the story, and it was too dangerous to try to drive from Baghdad to Mosul, where the alleged shootout was supposed to have occurred. Mike and I did the next best thing; we sat in the office and played cards. For hours we played cards. The rest of our team of photographers and engineers had gone to bed. Mike and I were often the last ones up. Through the years we've probably played more than five hundred hands of cards. I've won twice. Once I cheated, and the other time Mike let me win. Mike and I were about to start another hand of cards, as we sat in the office, when we heard a loud round of gunfire. It was close, too close. We'd both heard enough gunfire over the years to recognize when the sound was too close for comfort. Someone was shooting just outside our building. Actually, it sounded like our hotel was under attack.

"What should we do?" I asked Mike. With a deadpan expression, he looked me in the eyes and said, "What should we do? It's pretty obvious. Get under the table, call New

York, and finish our hand." We both burst into laughter. We might be in serious trouble, but Mike was making jokes. It's just what we both needed. Laughing allowed us to at least temporarily block out the anxiety we were both feeling. We did call New York. Our cameraman heard the gunfire as well, and he had managed to ease outside to videotape whatever he saw. What he saw were Iraqis celebrating in the streets of Baghdad. It was official: Saddam's sons were dead. As is the custom in that part of the world, men celebrated by firing their weapons in the air. It wasn't a crisis we were hearing—it was a celebration. A brief moment of laughter had kept us from panicking. We later filed our story. As it had so many times before, laughter had gotten me past a difficult moment.

Prayer, optimism, and laughter are all wonderful gifts. They are part of the foundation my mother used to raise her children. "If you pray hard, work hard, and treat people right, good things will happen," she often said. She left out laughter, but it was certainly vital. Her foundation was now mine. I've found that status or wealth can last but so long and take one but so far. Patience, prayer, optimism, and laughter are their own renewable-energy sources. Mix in a relentless work ethic, and you might be surprised how far you can go.

THIRTEEN

The Power of Forgiveness: When Father and Son Talk as Men

Forgive, and ye shall be forgiven.

—Luke 6:37

For if ye forgive men their trespasses, your heavenly Father will also forgive you.

—Matthew 6:14

CAN YOU TELL BY now that I'm an optimist? I choose to see the bright side of most any circumstance. My closest friends say I'm easygoing and almost never get visibly upset or angry. I carry my faith right out front and acknowledge that every good thing in my life has some connection to prayer, whether my own or someone else's. However, what is unseen is a heart that has been unwilling to forgive. I believe that God gives us power through our ability to forgive others and forgive ourselves. Nothing has drained me more of that power than my knot of unforgiveness. Like anger and fear, it kept me safe or, to my thinking, kept certain dangers at a distance. When TV's Tony Soprano said one of his enemies was "dead to me," I could totally relate. If someone crossed me personally or professionally, I would kill them off emotionally. I think that's one reason my anger never turned to violence.

I remember when a distant cousin offered me heroin when I was about eight years old. I got mad and never went to his house again. I never talked to him again and I never told my parents. When a girlfriend in college went out with another guy, from the moment I found out I never spoke to her again, ever. Back in my midtwenties in the mid-1980s, a colleague at a local station (a nighttime assignment editor) sent an e-mail to our news director criticizing my work and making a few false accusations. I got a copy of his e-mail. I never confronted him, but I also never spoke to him again. Mind you, this was the man who gave me my news assignments every day, but for more than a year I would not speak to him. I would not call his name. If he addressed me, I'd simply look at him and walk away. Not the best way to cover the news—and it still surprises me that I didn't get fired. I guess someone else in the newsroom was praying for me.

I could not forgive myself either. I can still remember every blown live report, every story where I've been beaten by the competition. For the longest time I kept a video diary of my worst work. Fortunately, I lost that videotape. An unwillingness to forgive was perhaps the coating on the masks I've worn most of my life. Like a hard acrylic, it kept most people and most things from getting too close or close enough to hurt me. In many ways, learning to forgive has been harder for me than learning to read or learning to speak clearly. It took only twelve years for me to learn to read. Speaking finally became easy at twenty. Forgiveness seemed beyond my reach for the first forty-five years of my life, and I was okay with that, or so I thought. For the longest time, my life was littered with people I had killed off emotionally for one reason or another. But, for me, there was at least one body that needed to be recovered: my father.

The conversation with my father was the most-thought-out, researched, prayed-over conversation I'd *never* actually had. Probably as early as middle school, certainly in college, and every few weeks of adulthood, I'd rehearse "that conversation I'll finally have with Daddy." I had discussed it with everyone in my family. They all encouraged me, but I just never could bring myself to call him and do it. The whole birds-and-the-bees conversation had long passed us by. All the big "man-to-man" conversations I had already had with my mother. For the longest time, I struggled just to remember the sound of his voice. I never remember him congratulating me, saying he was proud of me, or ever wishing me well in school, in sports, or, for that matter, in life. I wanted no part of him. My last significant conversation with my father was when I was about twenty-five years old.

Baltimore wasn't that far from Norfolk, where I was working at the time, so I had gone up there to reconnect with old friends. Out of respect for my mother, I often avoided my father, but my brother asked me to stop by and see him. I did, but I did not look forward to the visit with the joy and excitement one usually has for a long-distance parent. I dreaded it. I spent an afternoon with my dad and his wife. He questioned me about all aspects of my life and my job, even spoke proudly of me and my professional accomplishments. But what I waited to hear and wanted to hear was some acknowledgment of how he had behaved when I was young. I wanted him to tell me he was sorry. But he didn't. When the afternoon came to an end and he talked about staying in touch, I told him, "When I was a boy, you had no time for me. Now that I'm a man, I have no time for you." I was snarling when I said it, while my heart was breaking. I'd rehearsed those two sentences over and over again. Even down to my facial expression.

Another conversation I had contemplated having with him was one that involved the kind of violence I had witnessed between my parents. Instead of the two of them scratching at each other, this time it would be me, Byron Pitts, grown man, slapping my father around, forcing him with my fist to listen. Truth be told, those conversations in my head never lasted long or wound up any place productive. I've seen enough in my own life to know violence (although it might offer some temporary gratification) is never the long-term answer.

For twenty years there was nearly silence between us. We had perhaps five phone conversations, but I thought about him every single day. I often wondered if he was watching me on television. When I got to the network, I began wearing a white cotton handkerchief in my jacket pocket every day because I remembered that he always wore one. It's my daily reminder of the man I will always wish I had known better. Every time I glanced down at that handkerchief, I'd think of him. Outwardly, I was successful, but, inside, I felt incomplete. I was burdened by my unforgiving heart.

In the end, there was nothing courageous about my decision to talk with my dad again. I was simply paying off a bet with two of my workout buddies from my church. Dave Anderson and Darryl Carrington are two deacons at St. Paul Baptist Church in New Jersey. We would meet at the YMCA a few times a week to lift weights and for fellowship. On more than a few mornings, Darryl and I had to encourage Dave to lower his voice when he'd recite Scriptures while doing squats or bench presses. He was scaring some of the other people in the gym. Strong as an ox, Dave could also be as loud as one.

One week we got into a discussion about regrets—things in our past that pained us but which we hoped there was still time to address. I mentioned my father. The three of us talked about strained relationships with our fathers, though I seemed to be the most bitter. Darryl talked about his battle with his weight. Dave spoke of his temper. We agreed to pray for one another. Then Darryl challenged me. "If I start to lose weight," he said, "you have to start the conversation with your father." I refused. Refusing that challenge was as easy as lifting a twenty-pound dumbbell. But Darryl was relentless. Every morning for weeks he'd bring up the bet. Finally, I gave in. To his credit, Darryl didn't shame me into it; he nudged and supported me. "Jesus died for us, He laid it all on the line, what are you willing to give up?" he'd say as a smile crept across his face. It is hard for a Christian to think selfishly when one ponders that kind of question. It actually can be a strength builder and can be applied to most of life's struggles. Who can explain why after years of encouragement from family and close friends, I finally took a challenge from a friend in a weight room to push me toward a talk I had both dreaded and longed for most of my life? I guess God truly can use any of us in any situation. A sweaty weight room was the place for me. Days later, I called my dad on the phone. He was surprised I called. So was I.

We met at the Renaissance Harborplace Hotel in Baltimore for breakfast, just me and my dad, in 2005. He was seventy-seven; I was forty-five. It was the first time we had spent this much time alone, just the two of us, ever. Then it hit me. I didn't really know this guy, and he didn't really know me. Even those first eleven years, we were rarely alone. During my childhood we would almost always be with my mom or my siblings, people at church, members of my Boy Scout troop, or baseball or football teammates, but rarely was it just the two of us. Through most of high school and all of college, we never spoke or saw each other. During high school football games, I could always look from the sidelines into the stands and find my mother and smile. Secretly, I'd also look for my father, but he was never there, or if he was, I never saw him. Even when my father remarried, if I saw him I also saw his wife, a lovely woman who often tried but failed to get us to settle our differences. She always seemed more generous with her time than he was. So with enough baggage to fill an ocean liner, Byron A. Pitts sat down with William A. Pitts.

"Good morning, sir, how are you?" I greeted my dad as if it was a business meeting. That was the "Clarice" in me: be polite no matter what. We shook hands. As affectionate as my upbringing was, I don't ever recall my dad hugging or kissing me or ever saying he loved me. The last photograph we took together, when I was a child, was Christmas day, 1973. I was thirteen. He didn't put his arm around me, and I certainly didn't touch him. Now as an adult, I'll hug a tree, a dog, or a stranger if we're posing for a photograph. I simply love touching the people I love. But the notion of hugging my father had always seemed as foreign a notion as speaking Chinese.

"Good morning, son. You look good. How's the family?" As long as I can remember, my dad's always been a pleasant man in public, with an air of elegance (not Park Avenue elegance, more Rampart Street in New Orleans after-dark elegance). This day was no different, except looking into his oval-shaped eyes, I saw a flicker of innocence and sadness I'd never noticed before. There we were, father and son, the same last name, the same blood—we even look somewhat alike. Both six feet one, both balding, he a few shades darker, the stride of a once-confident young man long gone. Yet we share the same awkward gait. And our hands; identical, even down to the few strands of hair above each knuckle and to the length and shape of our fingernails. But it was still as if we were from different planets.

I motioned him toward the elevator and the ride up to the restaurant. For the first time in my life, I was suddenly looking down on him. Age had bent his spine, rounded his shoulders a bit, and left him with a slight limp. Had he been in an accident? Was it some degenerative condition? Does he have any major medical issues? Is this how I'll walk in thirty

253

years? These and about a hundred other questions filled my head as we walked the forty yards from the lobby to the elevators. In the ride up one floor, not a word passed between us. We both looked straight ahead, studying the details of an elevator door without any significance other than as a focus for our discomfort. The doors opened and I ushered him out first, touching the middle of his back. I wanted to put my arm around his shoulder. As a boy and later as an adolescent, I was repelled by the idea of touching my father. Now, as a man, the boy inside me longed for the moment. I'd seen fathers and sons do such things in the movies, at ball games, and at church. Each time, I had longed for the same moment, but when my chance came, I let it pass.

My father walked into the restaurant like a man out of place. His clothes and shoes hadn't appeared so worn when we stood in front of the hotel. Why was he still wearing his hat? When I was a boy, he always seemed so stylish. Now he looked like the man he'd been most of his life, someone who worked with his hands, unaccustomed to fine linens. He remarked in a surprisingly loud voice, "This is a fancy restaurant." This was the kind of restaurant I'd eaten in a hundred times over the course of my career. It was no big deal. I felt both a tinge of shame and unexplainable joy. I was finally standing with my poppa in public. We were in my world and one beyond his reach. We took our seats.

"Everything here is so expensive," he said, visibly uncomfortable.

"Please order whatever you'd like," I said, in as encouraging a voice as I could muster. Suddenly I couldn't breathe. "Please excuse me," I said and pushed away from the table and made my way to the restroom. Once behind closed doors, I splashed my face with cold water only to realize that my hands were shaking. I'm not one to succumb to nerves very often, but here I was on shaky legs with trembling hands. I could feel my heart pounding through my tailored sports jacket. I was a mess. After several deep breaths and a quick prayer—"Lord, be with me. Hold me in Your hands."— I returned to the table. My father appeared so engrossed in his menu he hardly noticed I'd been gone.

"What are you having, son? I don't know what I want," he said, expressionless.

"I'm going for the buffet. When the waiter comes, please order whatever you'd like." I'd never fully appreciated the value of comfort food until that moment. I crowded my plate with smoked salmon, strawberries, blueberries, and grapes, oatmeal and brown sugar—all my favorites but in unusually large portions. Much to my disappointment, I was uneasy being alone with him. I'd felt more comfortable with convicted killers and Afghan warlords than I did with my own father. Perhaps they could hurt me physically, but this man could wound me emotionally like no other. In desperate need to gain control, I decided to sit across from my father, as if he was just another interview on a run-of-the-mill story. He could have been a politician, a corporate executive, or a criminal. I'd decided to fill the time with as many questions void of any emotion for as long as possible.

"So how's your health? Are you a fan of the Baltimore Ravens [they were the Baltimore Colts the last time he and I were alone together]? Doesn't the Inner Harbor look nice?" Meaningless questions fired off with machine-gun frequency. I barely paused long enough to give the man a chance to answer. I'd leave no room for silence. Silence was awkward, and the occasion was already awkward enough. The silence left space for feelings and emotions, and I wanted no part of that.

"Your order, sir." Thankfully, the waiter interrupted with my father's breakfast. My goodness, it was a heart attack special: scrambled eggs, white toast with a small mountain of butter, hash browns, slices of bacon, ham, *and* three sausage links, with a cup of coffee. He looked pleased. I felt sorry for his arteries. Now my father was ready to push back, take control of the conversation.

"How's the family? How's work? Where have you been lately?" His questions were as pointless as mine. Then the conversation shifted. "So can you lend an old man some money?" I shifted uncomfortably in my chair. I was no longer nervous. "You know your old man is getting up in age. Now that you're doing so well, I'm sure you can help me," he said, with a big toothy grin. It was an odd sight, no one else in our immediate family could ever gin up that kind of smile. Maybe we weren't related after all. I wanted to shut him down, refuse him point-blank, and leave. Not this time.

"How much, Daddy?" I said, more resigned than angry or even annoyed. "A few thousand bucks would be nice." As the words left his lips, I flashed back to a painful moment from my childhood. This is the same man my mother had to take to court in order to make him pay seventy dollars per month to provide for his two sons after their divorce. I remembered the shame of being in court, my mother making sure my brother and I were dressed in our Sunday best. My father showed up with his girlfriend and his youngest son, Myron, insisting he couldn't afford the money because he had "other responsibilities." Thirty years later, he was asking me for a few grand with the same tone a co-worker might ask a colleague to borrow their stapler.

I felt something odd. The edges of my mouth were slowly turning up. I was smiling. It was the same menacing smile I'd seen on the face of bullies just before they pounced. Or the knowing smile of Wile E. Coyote as he was about to devour the Road Runner. This was my opportunity to savage this old man, belittle him with three decades of anger and shame. Instead, for reasons I can't easily explain, and in a modest tone reserved for reading Scripture during a church service, I said, "Daddy, I'm not here to give you money." His face fell a bit, but I just kept going. "I'm here to talk to you, man to man. I want you to know something. I want you to know a few things. I love you. I've always loved you and wanted you to love me. I've never felt your love, and for most of my life I've felt cheated. I've been angry. Everything I've done I did in part to prove to you I was worthy of your love." A lifetime of hurt and anguish and anger were pouring out of me like well water from my grandmother's old bucket.

I felt lighter with each word. "Daddy, I want you to know I'm not that angry little boy anymore. People who love me have forgiven me time and time again. God has forgiven me more times than I can count. I can't seek forgiveness unless I can give forgiveness. So, Daddy, I forgive you. I forgive you with all my heart." I never took my eyes off his face. At one point, I put one hand on top of his and used my other hand to grip the edge of the table for balance. Near the end, my voice cracked a bit. But I held on. I stopped talking, took a heavy breath, and smiled.

My father sat back in his chair, wiped his mouth with his napkin, then leaned in toward me. I leaned in to him. Might this be the moment we embrace? Would he whisper some pearl that would change the trajectory of my life? For the first time during all of breakfast his eyes met mine. Was the moment I'd longed for about to occur? He put down his fork, cleared his throat of scrambled eggs, and said, "So you're not going to give me the money?" As my mouth slowly dropped, he continued, "Then can I taste that," as he pointed toward the smoked salmon on my plate. By now my jaw and heart were falling in the same direction. Without thinking, I motioned down at the salmon and said, "Sure, it's yours." He smiled in appreciation.

That was it? The moment I'd convinced myself would change my life had come and gone. As I often do in an awkward moment, I dropped my head a bit and put my hand to my mouth like a student in class who'd just made a startling discovery. Then suddenly I was back in my father's car. I was a little boy again. Stone-faced. Expressionless. Then something odd happened. The passenger side door of my father's old Buick opened, and I got out. What happened next surprised me. I burst out laughing. Then I smiled. It was an earlobe to earlobe smile. I clapped my hands and continued to laugh. The couple at the next table looked a bit startled. It was in that moment that the last few pounds of what had felt like an unbearable weight lifted from my shoulders and across the width and length of my back. All my life I had been waiting for some miraculous healing moment, and that was it? It actually made me laugh when I realized that I didn't need my father to release me from the pain. With God's grace, I could release myself. For the first time, I no longer felt inadequate. I no longer felt inferior. I no longer had anything to prove.

In that moment, it felt as if I'd been born again. I had finally let go and it felt good. It felt better than good. It reminded me of my own baptism at the age of twelve, when I was submerged in water. I remember the weight of the water as it covered my body and the fear I felt as water filled my nostrils. My pastor used one hand to brace my back and the other to hold my hands against my chest when he dipped me in the pool behind the pulpit of our church. When he raised me out of the water, I squealed with relief. The weight was gone. Those seconds after my father's words reminded me of my baptism.

Sitting in the restaurant of the Renaissance Harborplace Hotel in my beloved hometown, I was suddenly enjoying a moment and was unwilling to let it go. I've never laughed longer. I reached across the table and touched my father's cheeks. He looked puzzled and said nothing. "Thank you! Thank you, Lord," I said again to the distraction of the couple next to us. "Thank you, Lord, for lifting this burden," I said, with my head tilted slightly back and my hands raised above my shoulders. All these years, and the answer to my anger had been right there, right where the answer to every question in my life had always been.

In that moment, sitting across from my father, I stepped out on faith, not in the words I had long rehearsed but in the words God had placed in my heart. I could finally stop beating this man up and, more important, stop beating myself up. My dad wasn't a great father, but he did what he did and that was okay. I'd always had a Father who loved me and valued my life, a heavenly Father, who'd been there for every ball game, every disappointment, and every achievement. This man sitting across from me was just that, a man. As I watched him finish his meal, all of what he had meant began to flood my memory. Like everyone else in my path, God had His reasons for our relationship to be what it was. God doesn't make mistakes. How many times had my mother told me that? So there was no reason for this man to apologize. No reason for him to even acknowledge my selfish offer of forgiveness.

Instead of being angry with my father, I wanted to thank him. Thank him for the things he did do and even the things he'd never done. He never abused me physically or emotionally. He never said a particularly unkind word to me. This man born in the segregated South with little more than a high school education had taught me things in both words and actions no college or university could ever teach. Like my mother, he was a hard and reliable worker. That was his gift. He had a curiosity about life, and perhaps that too was a part of my DNA. For the years my parents were married, my father was the one avid reader in the house, newspapers and magazines mostly. Perhaps he had more to do with my career choice than I'd ever given him credit for. For all the tears he caused, he had the ability to make people laugh. He was good at pleasing people, if only in short spurts. He wasn't a monster, just a man. He was the one who first introduced me to football, which had long been one of the great loves of my life. How many times had football kept me sane, kept me out of trouble? The game of football had given me a stiff measure of discipline, confidence, and social significance that helped fill the void of my father's emotional and physical absence. For all the years and all the things I blamed him for, there were reasons to show him gratitude. For the first eleven and a half years of my life, I lived in his house, ate his food, lived a modest working-class lifestyle.

We finished breakfast, and I walked him outside and waited as the valet brought up his car. I tipped the valet and gave my father the rest of the cash in my pocket, about forty dollars. We shook hands, I touched his face again and walked away. He drove off, the sound of his muffler eventually disappearing in the distance.

I wish I could say that was the beginning of a wonderful relationship. It wasn't. We talk from time to time. He still asks for money, and my answer remains about the same. But things are dramatically different. I am no longer angry at the man. I see him in a different light. I can see God's goodness even in him. I finally accepted that his relationship with my mother was their relationship. They were right that day in the car, when I was a boy, outside his girlfriend's house. I had nothing to do with their troubles. He is no longer the fuel that gets me going in the morning or drives my personal or professional ambitions.

Admittedly, it was tough letting go of the anger. It was like the first few weeks of wearing contacts after years of wearing glasses. I felt naked without my glasses. That thin piece of glass provided a nice wall between me and the outside world.

Anger had provided the same kind of protection. It kept the world at a distance and a frightened boy safe. I even worried for a time whether I could function without it. I had never considered my own anger as destructive but rather as instructive. I knew God was the real source of my strength, but anger was like a set of jumper cables. It provided a boost in the moments when I felt estranged from God. When I finally said the words "I forgive you" to my father, it freed me.

The Bible speaks of the power and the necessity for forgiveness. Jesus said we should cast the wrongs of others "into the sea of forgetfulness." I'm not there yet, but I'm gaining ground. I still keep score but no longer feel compelled to punish my opponent or relish their struggle. I'm not angry today; I'm grateful, fully grateful for the many blessings God has given me. There's a banquet of blessings for all of us. I still have my struggles. As a minister I know is fond of saying, "We all have skeletons in our closet, and some still have meat on the bone." Some of mine are still fully dressed. That's okay too. What are the things you struggle with? Where in life do you feel inadequate? Whom would you like to forgive? If you step out on nothing, you may be amazed at what you may find.

My wife remarked once with a smile in her voice, "Don't tell me God ain't good. He took a boy who couldn't read and put him on *60 Minutes*." We laughed. We laughed in part because hearing such terrible diction coming out of the mouth of a Stanford-educated woman with a brilliant mind was comical. But my life and the people who've blessed it, do speak to the power of God's grace. There are grand stories of men and women who pulled themselves up by their own bootstraps to achieve great things. That is not my testimony. I've been fortunate to grab on to the boot laces of others, and they were kind enough to pull me along. There are world-class athletes with phenomenal physical gifts who through shared effort and opportunity have set records and achieved greatness. That is not my testimony.

As an individual, there is nothing remarkable about my abilities or my intellect. I was simply blessed to be born in the greatest country on earth and blessed to have been surrounded by wonderful people who stood in the gap at every vital moment in my life. They, too, are ordinary people, and most readily admit they serve an extraordinary God. I'm not smart enough or wise enough to advocate a religion to anyone, but I know what's worked for me. I know that in all the darkest, loneliest moments of my life, when I felt the world was against me and the winds of conventional wisdom were in my face, in those moments, God held me in the palm of His hand. His Son, Jesus Christ, died so I might live. His sacrifice set the stage for every success I've been blessed to achieve thus far. When to the outside world it appeared I was stepping out on nothing, I was standing in the center of God's hands. He's got big hands. There's plenty of room.

Next to Scripture, my mother's sage advice, and my grandmother's wisdom, there are few words that move me more than Maya Angelou's poem "Still I Rise," especially the line "I am the hope and the dream of the slave." As an African-American man that line speaks to the trajectory of my life. The connectedness of unnamed generations marked with grand achievements, setbacks, and days of little consequence. But it is a journey forever moving forward. Regardless of one's race or ethnic identity, we are all on a journey. Who knows what the Lord has in store for me or for any of us. I'm more excited about the journey than I've ever been. I recently discovered my purpose. When I was a boy, my grandmother prophesized I'd become a preacher. She had high hopes for me. My mother always believed I could and would do great things. Thus far, being a parent, a husband, a brother, and a child have been the greatest accomplishments of my life. But I now know my purpose. I know it with the same clarity I knew as a child that I would one day learn to read. God put me here for two reasons: be a storyteller and be an encourager. I have friends who are avid runners, and few things bring them more joy than running outdoors with the air stroking their faces and the rhythm of their heartbeats as they take each step. It's that same joy I feel whenever I have the opportunity to tell a story or encourage someone else. All the struggles with literacy and speech, and even the difficulties in my relationship with my father, were placed in my path to teach me, to prepare me for my purpose: to encourage someone else to overcome their obstacles.

There is a purpose for all of us and a path for each of us to follow. Every path has a few potholes, and some of those potholes look like craters. There is a burden each of us must carry. My grandmother would also say, "God doesn't put heavy burdens on weak shoulders." My mother's response would always be, "Then God must think I'm a twin." She was trying to be funny. Her point was that she often felt she was carrying a burden meant for someone else. My mom might tell a few jokes or even rest a bit, but eventually she'd just take a deep breath and push on. Today, when I visit my mother down in North Carolina, we often sit on her porch, just me, her, and her dog. No matter where the conversation starts, it almost always goes back to those days when she struggled to raise her three children practically on her own. She'll remember something that will make her angry. Fast-approaching eighty years old, she's still fiery. But the anger passes. Then she'll remember something that will make her laugh. Almost always, she'll remember a day long gone that will make her eyes water: whether it's the memories of a day of financial hardship or a day she felt emotionally spent. They've never been tears of sadness but rather tears of gratitude and tears of amazement at what God can do. My mother taught me many things. Perhaps, most important, she taught me less with words and more by the way she's lived her life. She taught me that in times of uncertainty, step out to a place where only God is. Step out on nothing, and it will take you far. Safe journey.

FOURTEEN

Earthquake in Haiti: When Life Is Unfair

Be strong and courageous. Never be discouraged for our God is with thee always.

—Joshua 1:9

January 12, 2010

It was a slow news day—I had just finished an interview for an upcoming report on *60 Minutes* and I decided to head home early. I was just a few steps from the subway station at Columbus Circle in Midtown Manhattan—any second my cell phone would be useless and no one could reach me. A smile inched across my face. That's when my cell phone rang. It was Bill Felling, national editor for *CBS News*. Bill usually only called for one of two reasons: a possible golf game or breaking news. "A big earthquake just hit Haiti. I want you to go. Now!" Bill rarely wastes time on pleasantries—direct and honest is his style. "On it," I responded. With that, Bill said "I will call you back with particulars." For the next several hours I packed and talked on the phone with producer

Rodney Comrie (my partner on this assignment), all with an eye on cable TV for the latest news. "This is just awful," my wife Lyne said as she helped me get ready. How awful she and I and the rest of the world would soon find out.

The 7.0 earthquake struck Haiti with unforgiving force at 4:53 P.M. EST—a time of day when adults were still at work and many children were still in school. The epicenter was near the town of Leogane, approximately sixteen miles west of the capital city of Port-au-Prince. Phone lines were down, cell service was null, and the one airport was closed. Except for Twitter and Facebook, almost all of Haiti was cut off from the outside world. In many ways getting to the front lines of the wars in Afghanistan or Iraq was now logistically an easier task.

We flew first to Haiti's neighbor to the east, the Dominican Republic, in hopes of getting to Haiti by car from there. The airport in Santo Domingo was quickly filling up with media from around the world. Portable satellite dishes in large cases and camera equipment of every model lined the baggage claim area; clusters of men and women lined the curbside, negotiating prices for almost every means of transportation from airplanes and helicopters to minivans and SUV's. Soon enough our team from CBS was chest deep in the middle of it, yelling with the best of them. All the while, little more than two hundred miles away, thousands of people were dead or dying, and here stood people haggling over prices for transportation. But we had a job to do, and we managed to barter two old Toyota minivans for our trip. Since no one in our team spoke Creole, we smiled, pointed, and gestured our way to Port-au-Prince, making it to the border at about 6:00 P.M.

EST just in time to file our first report on the relief aid pouring into the country.

I've been to more than my share of disasters around the world, so I thought I was prepared for what I saw in Haiti. *It couldn't be as bad as the tsunami in Indonesia,* I said to myself. It wasn't—Haiti was worse. My *CBS News* colleague Harry Smith described it as well as anyone in one of his early reports. "What you saw in Indonesia was the absence of life (most victims were either washed out to sea or buried alive). In Haiti you are surrounded by death." And that's what you saw the moment you entered the capital city: Row after row of the dead. In some neighborhoods, bodies lined the road for as far as you could see. Most were uncovered. You could see where some lost their shoes, or shirts or pants, and some were virtually naked. I rarely looked at faces. Looking at faces was too emotional, and there was too much work to be done. So I usually stuck to the feet, but the tiny feet of children mixed in with the adults would always make my throat tighten. In time the smell was more difficult to manage than the sights.

According to the Haitian government more than 250,000 died, at least 300,000 thousand were injured, and 1 million were homeless. Government buildings collapsed. Schools were destroyed. Countless homes crumbled and in each case almost everyone inside was killed. Rich or poor, young or old, no group was spared. One group that fared well in the earthquake was Haiti's prison population. When the quake hit, inmates by the hundreds poured out of the main prison and blended into the broken landscape. For days and into weeks recapturing these convicts wasn't high on anyone's to-do list. Law-abiding citizens died by the thousands, all the while the lawless lived to steal and harm another day.

Of all the images I saw that first week the one that will always stand out most was the scene at the General Hospital, Haiti's largest public hospital. Much like the rest of the town, the hospital was destroyed in the quake—no one seemed to know how many patients, doctors, nurses, and staff died. Survivors were moved to a courtyard about half the size of a football field, where they would fight to stay alive alongside the injured, who arrived en masse every hour. After awhile, space was so limited that some patients were placed two or three to a bed and wooden doors were used as beds and gurneys. Only those with the most severe injuries were treated first. Most injuries were crush wounds—leg and arm fractures mostly—and the safest treatment option was relatively simple: amputation.

The first wave of incoming doctors to assist the tiny handful of Haitian physicians at the General Hospital were from neighboring countries in the Caribbean. The first several waves of physicians showed up bringing their knowledge and compassion, but very few if any medical supplies. You could see the frustration in their eyes as they wanted to help patients but simply didn't have the equipment. It would take days for basic medical supplies to reach the facilities. We're not talking fancy supplies and machines, just the basics.

Two of the first American physicians to arrive at the General Hospital were a husband and wife team from Massachusetts, Dr. Mark Hyman, a bestselling author and family physician, and his wife Dr. Pier Boutin, a noted orthopedic surgeon. They were soon putting in eighteen to twenty-hour days, performing one surgery after another. And without electricity, Dr. Boutin made her evening rounds using a cheap head lamp. In daylight I watched as she and Dr. Hyman and others amputated limbs with old hacksaws. "This looks like civil war medicine," I noted to Dr. Hyman. "It is," he said. "We're making use of whatever we have." That included a donated bottle of vodka for disinfectant since there was little alcohol. One evening, as the American team was caring for the sick and injured, something magical took place that spoke volumes about the Haitian spirit. On this particular evening, physicians like their patients were exhausted. There was little movement in the courtyard. Those who could slept; doctors on duty attended to the most severely injured while other patients mostly moaned—the sounds were haunting. But all of a sudden the courtyard seemed to go quiet. A woman who had been moaning earlier started to hum. Her voice washed over this pond of human anguish. I didn't recognize the tune, but there was a spirit to it. Then she started to sing. The man next to her joined in. Then the person next to him. Soon they had a small choir of people with minor to severe injuries singing along. They were singing the Haitian national anthem. Like all other national anthems, this speaks of courage and strength. Pride and dignity. In the midst of the worst natural disaster in their nation's history and most certainly the darkest hour of their own lives, these men and women managed the strength to sing in defiance of all they and their country had endured. That night I hummed that same tune as I fell asleep. It may have been the only time I smiled during my two weeks in Haiti.

Whenever I return from a trip like this I'm always most

grateful for family and friends. This time around, I was especially thankful to come home in time to say good-bye to one of my dearest friends. Peter Holthe had been fighting a rare and deadly form of cancer valiantly for nearly two years. In February 2010 his wife, Kara, had e-mailed me. Pete's time was winding down so I should come and see him. On the evening of February 13, Kara picked me up at the subway station near their home just outside of San Francisco. She greeted me with a warm hug and her familiar smile. "You and Pete should enjoy this time together," she said with a sense of sadness in her voice. When I walked in their house I understood. Pete was in a hospital bed set up in their living room. Always a big fellow, a few inches above six feet and well north of two hundred pounds, Pete had lost considerable weight. But he was still strong physically and spiritually. "Baby boy," he screamed when he saw me. We hugged like schoolgirls. (Pete could always give great bear hugs.) Despite his failing health he was still strong. Pete's parents and siblings and Kara's brother were all in town. They, along with hospice, were providing Pete with twenty-four-hour care. I greeted everyone and turned my attention back to Pete. I sat next to Pete's bed, we held hands, our foreheads almost touching; we were close enough to whisper and hear the other clearly. "I'm dying baby boy," Pete said his voice a bit raspy. "But no time soon." We both laughed. "Would you pray for me?" Pete asked. I had known this brilliant man for nearly thirty years, discussed almost every topic two friends could discuss, but Pete had never asked me to pray for him. Pete called Kara over and we prayed. I started reciting the same prayer Clarice taught me years ago that day after she and Dad fought on the street in Baltimore.

The mood in Pete and Kara's living room was similar to the mood many nights when my mother came to my bedroom to pray. A sense of sadness, exhaustion, and humility along with an unending hope better days lay ahead. "Dear wise and almighty God we come to you as humbly as we know how just to say thank you Lord. Thank you Lord for blessings seen and unseen. . . ." I'm not sure about Kara, but Pete and I were crying. Tears of both sadness and joy. Sad for obvious reasons. Joy because we could be together one more time. After we prayed, Kara went back to the kitchen. Pete and I went back to whispering. We talked sports. We talked world events. We told war stories from college. We talked about our children and our spouses. Pete assured me Kara was taking great care of him. Then Pete told me "I'm getting tired baby boy. You take good care. We've come a long way since OWU. We've done okay. I will see you again sometime, somewhere. I love you." "I love you baby boy," were the only words I could get out. We kissed the other's cheek. Then Pete surprised me. He pulled my neck hard. Pulled my head to his mouth and whispered so gently. "Now you know Kara is NOT taking you back to the train station. I want her here with me." He released my neck, winked, and smiled. I took a cab back to my hotel, leaving Pete with the people he loved, and who loved him most. To be surrounded by his spouse and family, that's all Pete wanted in the end. It's probably true for most of us.

Pete died two weeks later. He was fifty. During his memorial service family and friends spoke. His baby brother told stories that at times made your stomach hurt from laughing and at other times you could feel your heart breaking. What was most touching was how profoundly Pete had touched so

many people in similar ways. His brilliant mind. His wit. His
boyish charm. Not a day passes that I don't think about Pete.
By the time you reach a certain age we all begin to lose people close to us. Somehow knowing that doesn't make it any
easier. But I am comforted by the words of Dr. Seuss, "Don't
cry because it's over. Smile because it happened." When I
think of Peter Holthe I will always smile.

The loss of life in Haiti and the loss of my dear friend
Pete are just two reminders that life isn't always fair, but it *is*
precious. A gift we get to hold but only for so long. We can
never own it outright, but rather savor it, maximize it for a
brief time.

Epilogue

SHE WAS AN IMMIGRANT from Haiti who had lived with the shame for thirty-six years. He was a prominent banker who wiped tears from his eyes as he admitted the truth about his adult son. They were telling me their stories because they knew that I would understand. I shared their secret and their pain. A history of illiteracy. But we shared something much greater. We were survivors. We had triumphed over a debilitating and shameful struggle despite tremendous odds against us.

For two years now, I've been traveling the country lecturing on illiteracy and the difficulties I've had to overcome. The stories I've heard have saddened and heartened me. We are the most educated nation in the world. But we have a staggering rate of illiteracy. If you think you don't know someone who is illiterate, think again. Perhaps you have an older relative who calls you to write things down because he or she "can't find my glasses." Or perhaps you know someone who is grateful for the car GPS because, truthfully, they can't read a map or written directions.

As an adult, imagine hiding for a lifetime something so fundamental to your everyday life. Never able to fill out a job application or take a driving test. Imagine raising children who have read more books than you. If you're a child, what about taking homework home from school and never understanding it. Or experiencing the humiliation of being caught by your friends. How do you start your education over? In whom do you confide? These are questions I faced as a young teenager. But today I'm an avid reader. Books are a lifeline, and words are the foundation of my professional life.

People laughed at me when I told them I wanted to work in television. It might have seemed impossible, since I could barely speak. But in my silence and beneath my shame, I had a burning belief that all things are possible. A faith that God would make a way. I think there are lessons to be learned from my journey and the steps I took, even as a child, to put myself on a path to success: self-discipline, hard work, the power of prayer. The importance of finding and nurturing mentoring relationships. My story may be no different from yours or someone you know. I want to encourage you to have faith, to believe in the impossible.

I also want to encourage the "angels," like my Dr. Lewes. I've met them all across the country at luncheons and dinners. They speak to me through tears about their challenges and often thankless responsibilities in trying to bring light to a world without words. They tutor, they read, they fund-raise, and they encourage. They need to believe in the difference they are making in people's lives and in this world. And they must know how much we love and appreciate them. (I would not have made it through college without my buddy Peter Holthe.)

There are also countless people who have shared their personal stories or told me about their children. I wrote this book to celebrate our victories and the successes of so many like us. I wrote this book for the adults who are faking it, for the children who are being left behind, and for every child who sits in the basement class in his or her school, labeled "slow" or "unteachable" when, in fact, they may be hiding an inability to read.

In 1978 I was on the verge of dropping out of college. In 2006 I was invited to Ohio Wesleyan as their commencement speaker. Cap and gown, doctor of humane letters, the whole deal. What an improbable journey. It happened to be Dr. Lucas's final commencement. He was retiring. I had always wondered what I might say or do if he and I ever crossed paths. When the moment came, I braced my back, took a deep breath, looked him in the eye, and said, "Thank you, Dr. Lucas. I would not be here without you. Bless you." Then I took his hand, gripped his shoulder, and said, "I wish you well." He smiled. I couldn't be sure if he even remembered me. He'd served a valuable purpose in my life. Nothing more. Nothing less. That day as part of my speech, I told the story of my experiences with Dr. Lucas. I never mentioned his name. The goal wasn't to embarrass him, but rather to share that part of my journey with the graduating class; success is often preceded by struggle.

Just as it was on my first day of college, little was going as planned. It was mid-May, but it felt like mid-November in Ohio. It was cold and rainy. The graduates and their guests were soaked. But adversity and I were old friends by now, and it was time for the commencement speech. So I took the "opportunity" God had given me and made the best of it. Here's some of what I had to say that chilly day:

I know many of us prayed for sunshine and clear skies today, but thank the Lord He made umbrellas. To the graduates, President, Faculty, staff, the Board of Trustees, honored guests: It's a privilege to be with you today as we mark this historic moment in the life of our beloved university, and the lives of these young people. As uncomfortable as conditions may be, we're still blessed. It's Mother's Day. There are few gifts greater one could give a mother than to fill her cup, fill her heart with pride. Graduates, many of you may not have a dollar in your pocket, but the gift you've given your families today is priceless. . . .

I know we've come to honor the ones receiving the degrees today. But I believe graduations are also moments to honor those who paid for those degrees. Graduates, despite what some of you may think, you did not get here by yourselves. I would ask the parents, grandparents, aunts, and uncles—anyone who made a tuition payment and prayed a prayer for one of these children—to please stand. Parents and relatives of the class of 2006, please stand so we can applaud you. This is also your day. I'd especially like to acknowledge the single parents here this afternoon. As a father, I know it's not easy for two parents to raise a child. But as the proud baby boy of a single mother, I too know the unique sacrifices that single moms and dads make. On behalf of your sons or daughters, thank you for your many sacrifices.

I'd like to thank my own mom, who, just as she did twenty-four years ago, sits in the audience today, beaming with pride. My mother, Clarice Pitts.

A newspaper reporter interviewed my mom once for a story about me and asked, "Mrs. Pitts, how did you manage as a single parent, a divorcée, to send three kids to college?" Her answer: "It was simple. I said, 'Go to college, or I will beat you to death.'"

Simple parenting is good parenting. Thanks, Momma. I'd also like to thank my brother and his family for joining us today. . . .

Let the record show I believe in Ohio Wesleyan University. The liberal arts education provided here is second to none.

Graduates, please know you are well qualified to compete in any field, against any competitor, from any college, at any place in the world.

As a correspondent for CBS News, I've interviewed the last five presidents of the United States, reported from thirty-three countries, covered three wars and natural disasters of biblical proportions, from the tsunami in Indonesia to Hurricane Katrina in New Orleans. None of that would have been possible had it not been for the four years I spent here in Delaware. Not possible without professors like Verne Edwards, the head of the journalism department until his retirement. Mr. Edwards is here today with his lovely bride, Dolores. Thank you, Verne. Can I call you Verne now? For four years I was always nervous just to be in your presence. Today I'm grateful to call you my friend.

None of the dreams I had for my life would have been possible if not for many of the friends I made at OWU. Friends like Peter Holthe from Minnetonka, Minnesota. Pete was the whitest white guy I'd ever met. We were hallmates in Thomson Hall freshman year and suitemates sophomore year in Welch Hall. Pete told me that before we met, the only black people he'd ever seen were in Ebony magazine. Pete and I remain close to this day. That's the beauty of OWU. Children of the working class and children of the wealthy can meet in this corner of the world to learn of history's great philosophers while studying the forces that went into making an igneous rock. I had a geology class (I hated geology and, for the most part, geology hated me). But my first time in the mountains of Afghanistan, the country was foreign yet the rocks beneath my feet were familiar.

Class of 2006, you are 401 strong. You represent 21 different countries of the world. You are 401 of the estimated 1.3 million college seniors graduating in America this spring. According to BusinessWeek, you are about to enter the best job market for college graduates in at least five years. You have much to feel good about. Feel confident but never arrogant. Arrogance, I believe, is the cloak of cowards. Stay humble. My mother always told us, If you work hard and pray hard and treat people right, good things will happen. But, above all else, stay humble. Humility has its place.

It is with that sense of humility I'd like to share a few

final thoughts with the class of 2006. I know all of you are smart and computer-savvy. In this computer information age, you laugh at people like me and your parents as we still struggle with the VCR back home, and you stay connected with your friends by Skype, Facebook, MySpace, and Xanga. What the heck does Xanga mean? I bet most of you own an iPod, laptop, and a cell phone. And all those gadgets are wonderful.

But when you leave this place, there are a few old-fashioned tools you're also going to need in order to survive in this ever-changing world. Here are two:

Please and thank you. Knowing how to give a Power-Point presentation may take you far. But human decency and politeness will make the landing easier when you get to wherever you're going. Please and thank you. Powerful words. Empowering words. Make them part of your permanent vocabulary. It worked for your grandparents. It will work for you.

If I had a speech title today, it would be "Follow Your Dreams and Find Your Passion." I believe in dreams. Progressing from academic probation during my freshman year at OWU in 1978 to Commencement speaker in 2006—I have to believe in dreams!

Whether you graduate today Phi Beta Kappa, Summa Cum Laude, Magna Cum Laude, or just plain "Thank you, Lord," you must believe in your dreams. You see, America is at a crossroads. We need new dreamers—not daydreamers but dreamers. Daydreamers play and procrastinate, but dreamers plan their work and work their plan.

So, my future fellow alumni, dream and dream boldly.

When good men and good women dream, a runner breaks the four-minute mile. An astronaut steps foot on the moon. A doctor finds a cure for a terrible disease. A colored girl from the segregated South becomes Secretary of State. . . .

Class of 2006, what is your role? What do you dream? And you can't dream without faith. Young people, degrees are good. But when trouble comes—and for you just entering the world beyond college, trouble will surely come—please know this. If you take one step, God will take two.

Have faith in something greater than yourself.

Now, I'm a Christian and proud of it. But whether you turn to a preacher or a priest, an imam or a rabbi, have a name you can call other than your own. You can't dream without faith. And faith without love is empty love.

Now, I'm not talking about that kind of love you think you may have found on Fraternity Row during freshman year or at your first party in the Cave. I'm talking the kind of love I've seen on the battlefields of Iraq and Afghanistan. It's the kind of love angels bring. It's the kind of love I experienced here at OWU, second term, freshman year. This is my testimony. I'm sure each of you has yours.

That term I was on academic probation. I had an English professor—for the record, he no longer teaches here.

To tell you how slow I was, I got a D in his class, first term, and took his class again the second term. This English professor knew me. I knew him. One day in class he handed out test scores in small blue notebooks, and when he handed me mine, he announced in a loud and clear voice to all my classmates, "Mr. Pitts, congratulations! Your best work thus far." With a bit of surprise and a sense of relief, I opened that blue book, and there at the top of the page, in bold letters, was a D+. Seeing my anguish, the professor leaned forward and said, "Mr. Pitts, come see me after class."

I did, and that English professor who no longer teaches here, said, "Mr. Pitts, may I speak frankly?" Before I could answer, he went on and said, and I quote (I carried this quote in my heart ever since). He said, "Mr. Pitts, your presence at Ohio Wesleyan University is a waste of my time and the government's money. I think you should leave."

"A waste of my time and the government's money." I was eighteen years old, and this man, this teacher, crushed my dreams. So taking his advice, I walked over to the admissions office and picked up papers to withdraw from school.

It was clear to me I was not worthy, so I sat outside Slocum Hall with tears running down my cheeks, filling out the forms to drop out of college. At that moment, a stranger walked by—a woman with a round face and a warm smile. She said, "Excuse me, young man, are you okay? May I help?" With nothing to lose, I explained my situation. She listened and said, "Come by and see me tomorrow. Do not leave school before talking with me." I would soon find out that this stranger, another English professor, was not just a professor. She was my angel.

Dr. Ülle Lewes, please stand. Dr. Lewes. That day you didn't simply soothe my tears. You saved my life. Thank you for believing in me when I didn't believe in myself. Thank you for being my angel.

Class of 2006, each of you have angels to thank for bringing you this far. I encourage you to thank each one. And don't just thank them. By being a high achiever you can *thank them. And you can thank them someday by being an angel for somebody else. Graduates, real success is not measured by how much you take from this life but by how much you give to it.*

For those of you going on to graduate school, I say, give yourself to your studies and study the way Michelangelo painted. For those beginning careers or just taking summer jobs, learn to work like Martin Luther King. Live each day as if it's your last. Don't simply be good—be better. Better isn't good enough, so be the best. Don't settle for your best. Be an angel.

If you haven't figured it out by now, I'm an optimist. I believe in each of you. I believe in the promise of America, despite her many warts. America is still the greatest country on earth. Be good to her and she'll be good to you. Love her and she'll love you back. Be dreamers and be passionate about your dreams.

I leave you with the words of Horace Mann, the founder of nearby Antioch College in Yellow Springs, Ohio. He told Antioch's first graduating class: "Be ashamed to die until you have won some victory for humanity."

To the graduating class of 2006 from Ohio Wesleyan University: Congratulations and God bless you. Today you make your family proud. Now go and make your world better—because you live.

Acknowledgments

This book would not have been possible without the kindness, patience, and hard work of many people and the whispered prayers of many more. I first would like to thank my wife, Lyne. Thanks to her, I married well. She's been an encourager and a confidant. When I needed a push, she gave it. When I needed a hug, she gave one. Thanks to my family of course. My beloved grandmother, Roberta Mae Walden, who left us in 2000. My mother, sister, and brother; my aunts Gladys, Diane, Rebecca and Pat, along with uncles Albert, Alton, Fred, and Luther; and my late cousin Marian Sanders. Thanks to Dr. Ülle Lewes, who is an honorary family member, and to Dorthey Daniels and Andre Jones, who are the best friends a person could ever ask for.

I want to express my gratitude to all of my friends and colleagues at *CBS News*, who have made the last twelve years of my professional life the most rewarding. A special thanks to producers Betty Chin and Rodney Comrie, who have traveled the country with me in search of important truths worth telling. I'm also grateful for the support of Jeff Fager, Sean McManus, Les Moonves, Bill Felling, Terri Stewart, Larry Doyle, and (the late) Martin Gill. Thanks as well to Richard Liebner at N. S. Bienstock, my agent and my friend.

This book would have remained just a dream without Jan Miller and the team at Dupree/Miller and Associates. My thanks especially to agent Nena Madonia. They were all an answer to my prayers. I'm so grateful to St. Martin's Press and my executive editor, Kathryn Huck. She has made the rough places smooth. I'd also like to acknowledge Howard Kurtz at the *The Washington Post,* because it was an article he wrote that set this project in motion, and Lisa Dallos, who believed in my story.

A special mention for college professor Verne Edwards and a dear friend in Boston, Maceo Vaughn.

To Daniel, Tiffani, Benjamin, Angela, Brittni, and Christiani, I hope I make you as proud as you make me.

And thanks to all of you who have allowed me into your homes and into your lives to tell your stories. You have taught me more than you will ever know.

Index